THE LANGUAGE OF THE HAND

THE LANGUAGE OF THE HAND

Being A Concise Exposition Of the Principles and Practice of the Art of Reading the Hand

BY WHICH

THE PAST, THE PRESENT, AND THE FUTURE

By
Henry Frith
and
Ed. Heron Allen

ILLUSTRATED BY DORA NOYES

GYAN

Published by

Gyan Publishing House
5, Ansari Road
Daryaganj, New Delhi-110002
Phone: 011-47034999, 9811692060
E-mail: books@gyanbooks.com

Distribution Network
gyanbooks.com
India, USA, Canada, UK, Australia, France

ISBN : 978-81-212-6198-2 (PB)
First Published, 1899

2nd Impression 2022

Printed at: Gyan Press, Delhi.

THE LANGUAGE OF THE HAND
Author: Henry Frith, Ed. Heron Allen

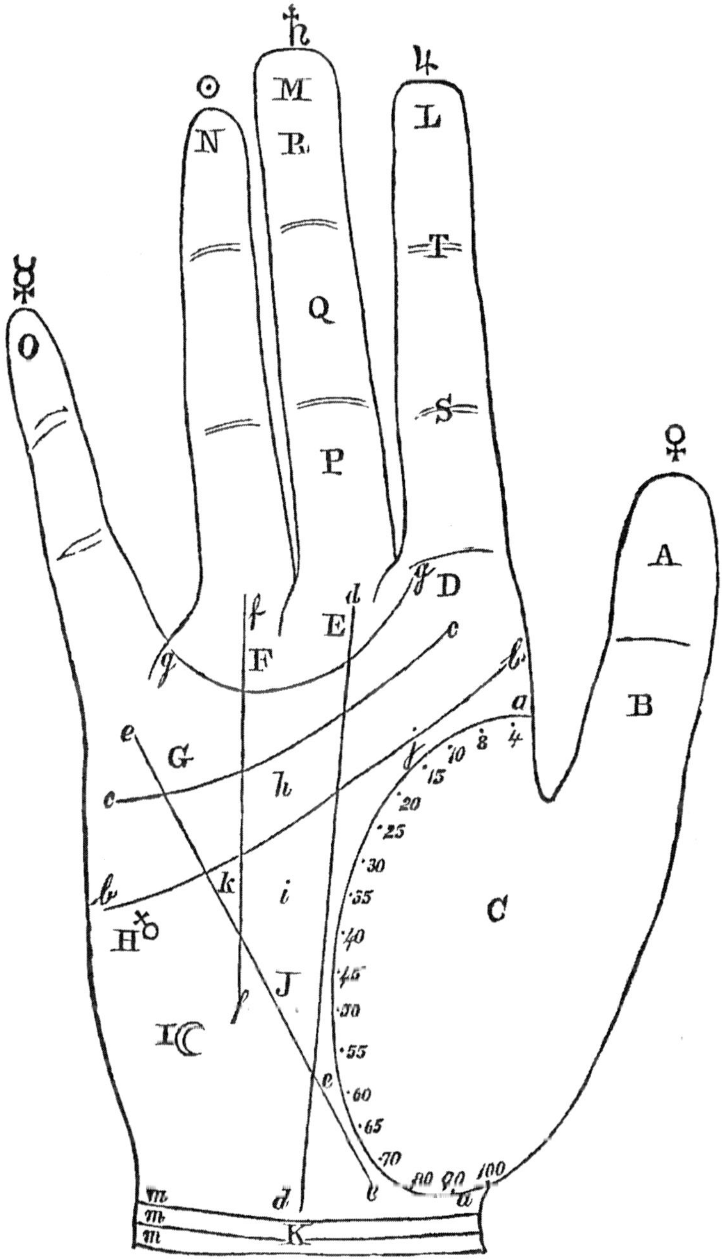

M
R
N
L
T
Q
O
S
P
A
D
E
F
G
B
H
C
J
I
K
4
8
10
15
20
25
30
40
55
60
65
70
80
90
100

EXPLANATION.

A. Will.
B. Logic.
C. The Mount of Venus.
D. The Mount of Jupiter.
E. The Mount of Saturn.
F. The Mount of the Sun.
G. The Mount of Mercury } The Percussion.
H. The Mount of Mars } The Percussion.
I. The Mount of the Moon } The Percussion.
J. The Plain of Mars.

a a. Line of Life.
b b. Line of Head.
c c. Line of Heart.
d d. Line of Saturn or Fate.
e e. Line of Liver.
f f. Line of the Sun or Fortune.
g g. Belt of Venus.

K. The Rascette.
L. Square finger.
M. Spatulate finger.
N. Conic finger.
O. Pointed finger.
P. The 1st Phalange.
Q. The 2nd Phalange.
R. The 3rd Phalange.
S. The 1st Joint (Order).
T. The 2nd Joint (Philosophy).

h. The Quadrangle.
i. The Triangle.
j. The Upper Angle.
k. The Inner Angle.
l. The Lower Angle.
m m m. The Bracelets of Life.

THE LANGUAGE OF THE HAND

BEING

A CONCISE EXPOSITION OF THE PRINCIPLES AND PRACTICE OF THE ART OF READING THE HAND

BY WHICH

THE PAST, THE PRESENT, AND THE FUTURE

MAY BE EXPLAINED AND FORETOLD

BY

HENRY FRITH

AND

ED. HERON ALLEN

ILLUSTRATED BY DORA NOYES

Dedication.

TO

C. M. F.

THIS WORK IS INSCRIBED

BY

The Author.

CONTENTS.

PREFACE.

Prius quam incipias consulto, et ubi consulueris mature facto opus est.
—*Sallust.*

CHIROMANCY, which includes Chirognomy, concerning which we propose to treat in the following pages, is of very ancient origin. The derivation of the word is from the Greek χείρ (the *hand*) and μαντεύομαι (I foretell). In fact, the Science is that which enables us to divine character, past events, and destiny from the shape, the mounds, and the lines of the hands.

There is more in this science than may at first sight appear to an observer. We know that certain bumps upon the head indicate certain characteristics of human nature. The colour of the hair and eyes, the form of the mouth, of the chin and nose, the shape of the ears, with other signs and attributes of person, and the general form of the body, nails, and fingers afford certain and infallible indications of temperament as varied as the forms of ear or face. Nothing in nature is more remarkable than the fact that, although every individual amongst the millions of living human beings possesses features, and organs of perception, visibly formed for the same purposes, and used for those purposes, no two persons possess them exactly alike. The variety therefore is infinite.

What, then, are we to say concerning the hand of

man? Character can be read from the features and expression of the face, why not from the marks and lines upon the hand? Because, you will say, the "horny-handed son of toil" will show you more and a greater variety of marks (not *lines*) than the idle man, or the individual who works with his pen, and not with spade, pickaxe, or hammer. We grant that the effects of manual labour will be different, but they will not produce the same lines. Put any two men at the same work, their hands will not be any more alike after a week's work than they were at the beginning of the week.

Neither are the lines in the hand caused by the general folding or construction; as an old writer puts it—*Deus et Natura nihil efficiunt frustra.* Certainly nothing has been made in vain, and why, then, should the lines of the human hand not bear some significance? "Nature," continues one old authority, "has impressed lines in the forehead which is not capable of restriction or plication, therefore this cannot hold, that the construction of the hands should cause the formation or appearance of lines in the hands; for between the joints of the fingers many persons have lines, and of different forms. Other people have very few—mayhap none at all—and here there is no flexion."

We therefore support the principle that there is a meaning attached to the lines and mounds of the hand, though we will not take upon ourselves to affirm unreservedly that the meanings attached to those lines or mounds are always unalterably the true ones, as far as the future is concerned. It is against reason and common sense to foretell, beyond power of mutation, events which cannot certainly be known to any human being. That certain identical lines and mounds are visible in the hands of individuals of like temperament is not to be gainsaid. Phrenology has given us standing ground for so much assumption in regard to Chiromancy. Lavater was a master in reading temperament from facial observation. The hand will afford as much information if we study it properly.

As to which hand should be inspected, it is the generally received rule that the left hand is the one which the Chiromant must study first, and that the indications which he finds in that hand must be modified or corrected by those found in the right; and this, it seems to us, is owing to the fact that the left hand is (except in the case of a left-handed subject) comparatively the idle hand, and is therefore the more adapted to the proper formation of the lines and mounds. We have found in an ancient authority a *manifestly absurd* rule which declares that it depends whether the owner of the hand had been born by night or by day; that if the former, the left hand is to be inspected, that in the latter case the right hand; though both are necessary for a complete divination. "*Nocte etiam natis sinistra magis favet, die vero et in aurora natis dextra, quamvis utraque manus probe inspicienda et examinanda est.*"

We shall recur to this in the body of the work, and therefore pass on to the consideration of the antiquity and history of Chiromancy, which will lead us to the practical chapters on the science.

It is impossible to ascertain the origin of Chiromancy, nor would it be of much practical use if we could do so. It has been stated that Homer wrote a treatise upon the science, but this is improbable on the face of it. The Romans appear to have been acquainted with Chiromancy; and Dryden, in his *Juvenal*, says—

> "The middle sort, who have not much to spare,
> To Chiromancer's cheaper art repair,
> Who clap the pretty palm to make the lines more fair."

Artemidorus, in the second century, wrote of Chiromancy, and we have many later authors, such as Cocles in 1504, De la Chambre 1653, with other Italian and French writers, as well as Germans, down to the lady who produced the "Grand Jeu de Société" in Paris.

The first regular work, however, upon this art or science seems to have been produced in the fifteenth century by Hartlieb, who produced a very remarkable and now very rare volume entitled "Die Künst Ciromantia." The date of this volume—a rare specimen of the block printing—is 1448. Cocles above mentioned appears to have made a study of Chiromancy, and it is recorded by the writer of the "Anecdotes de Florence," that he made some successful predictions from an observation of hands and features. Cocles himself was the victim of the murder he predicted, and fulfilled his former prophecy to the effect that he himself would die from the effects of a blow upon the head, which did actually cause his death. This prediction came true to the letter, as he was struck with an axe by the man whom he had connected with a "detestable murder," to be performed that very day.

The study of Physiology and Chiromancy (or Palmistry) were not uncommonly united, and many seers tried their hands at the art. We have found two very excellent professors, whose works, with other rather more modern and equally scarce pamphlets, we have laid under contribution in the following pages. We have devoted some years to the study of the subject, and, reading the palm as we do, we find much to recommend the art. There is considerable instruction to be gained by its practice, but we would recommend caution in fully interpreting the lines of the hand in public. There may well be occasions when silence even will best meet the case; for, putting aside the objection sensitive people may entertain on the subject, nervous individuals, and those whose minds are apt to dwell upon trifles as likely to affect their future happiness, should not be "operated on."

We have had experience of this in ordinary "fortune-telling," when "tears" fell to the lot of a lady three times successively, notwithstanding some good-natured attempts to alter Fate by shuffling the fortune-telling apparatus. The young lady was deeply impressed by the singular repetition of the unhappy fate in store for her, and did not recover her spirits for some days. As a matter of fact, her life since then—some fifteen years ago—has been singularly unhappy, full of disappointments and pain, mentally and bodily. The prediction was only too true.

But to resume. Chiromancy died out in the seventeenth century, when Physiognomy usurped its place, but within a few months Society has taken up the "craze," as it has been ignorantly called, for there is much more sense in the study of Chiromancy than in ninety-nine of the passing fancies taken up by people who have no time to take up anything. One ancient writer saith that Chiromancy "informeth us to know and discerne by the Hand the Complexions and Constitutions of Bodies; the Sufferings and Sorrows of Humane Life; the Felicity and Infelicity thereof; and, in fine, all things Good or Bad that may befal or betide Man or Woman." Most singular speculations may be drawn from the lines, he says; that is to say, "from their Longitude, Latitude, Profundity, Rectitude, Obliquity, Intersection, Application, Opposition, Conjunction, Separation, Continuity, Discontinuity, Proportion, Disproportion, Lucidity, Apparency, Pallidity, Rubedity, Fuscedity (which is a cloudy darkness of color), Mollicity," &c., from their "Position, Calligation, and Form."

Nor is this all that pertains to the correct reading of the hands: there are other indications which the student must take note of and remember, such as the crosses, stars, rays, and branches, ascensions and descensions, "right or torted;" so Palmistry is not the mere amusement it would appear. Granting, therefore, that these lines were put upon the hands by Nature, as indications of character, or as heritage from our parents and remoter ancestors, whose characteristics we naturally inherit, we shall be able to make certain diagnoses of the kind of people we are.

The explanation of these signs is named CHIROMANCY. "Onely this I shall tell you—the Author hath not onely in this small tract reduced all to a concise and Methodical Discourse," but "added divers others of his own observations."

"Seek and ye shall find!" said the greatest and highest Philosopher, but now and then to aid the feeble powers of man, to guide his erring but well-intentioned footsteps, Providence sends a man gifted with powers beyond those of his fellow-mortals, whose efforts, whose researches, and whose natural powers, help man a step farther towards that goal which is already in sight, towards that power which is only just out of reach of our grasp, towards that knowledge which is man's pre-ordained prerogative, but for which, in the days of our forefathers, its seekers were condemned to the prison, the torture, and the scaffold. Such men as this were Hermes Trismegistus, Apollonius, and Paracelsus, such men are and have been Gall, Lavater, D'Arpentigny, and Desbarrolles.

Gall and Lavater taught methods of divination complicated to acquire and difficult to put into practice. M. le Capitaine D'Arpentigny at length appeared on the scene, endowed with a cool judgment, an indomitable perseverance, and an unflagging watchfulness. The system he inaugurated, under the title of *Chirognomy*, though vague in places, became elucidated and enlarged as it passed through the hands and brains of such men as Bichat, Montaigne, Rabelais, Herder, and Balzac. To these men came Desbarrolles, with his sister science *Chiromancy;* what the former wanted, the latter supplied; what was confusing in the latter was explained by the former; and the twin doctrines uniting with their younger and necessarily more fallible satellite, *Graphology*, became a harmonious whole,—"The Science of the Hand."

Desbarrolles, having studied all the Chiromantic works on which the Sorcerers, Astrologers, Necromancers, and Charlatans of the Middle Ages founded their pretended knowledge, rejected all as the creations of unscrupulous mystery-mongers, and seeking for Chiromancy its true origin in the Kabbala of primitive India, embodied the principles of our science, by which the instincts of man, his past life, and, to a certain extent, his future may be explained and revealed.

We say "to a certain extent," for were we to say the absolute unavoidable future may be read in the hand, we should lay ourselves open to just condemnation for charlatanry and fatalism. What we do claim for the science is this, that by indicating, by means of the instincts and tendencies shown in the hands, the events which, if left to themselves, would supervene, such events, by the suppression of the tendencies which will bring them about, may be neutralized or avoided entirely.

Let us claim for this Opuscule the merit of opening your eyes to the tendencies of your nature, and the probable results of those tendencies. Let this brochure be the means by which you may so encourage your finer instincts, and so combat and neutralize your evil ones, that by attention to the aptitudes and weaknesses with which you entered this world, you may learn and labour truly to get your own living *in that state of life unto which it shall have pleased God to call you.*

INTRODUCTION.

"Facts are stubborn things!"

SOME time ago we were dining with some friends living in one of the most populous and popular suburbs of our great city. The other guests present were all people of a character unmistakably suburban, that is, they were composed for the most part of men whose business took them to town every week-day, to whom the suburbs, where their wives and families lived, moved, and had their being, was but a dormitory. Consequently, the business element largely prevailed, and the company, in which the sexes were evenly balanced, was of a nature decidedly practical, and one in which abstruse, or psychic questions would meet with but little sympathy, or unbiassed discussion. Our host introduced us, for the purpose of escorting in to dinner, to a lady whose personal appearance was indicative only of a careless, matter-of-fact disposition, capable of ridiculing or seriously discussing any question that might arise.

As we took our seats and our neighbour took off her gloves—

"I hope, Miss ——," we said, "we shall not bore one another, for I see you paint, and I don't.

I am musical, and I see that you are not; that is to say, that you prefer catchy melody to abstruse harmony—that you prefer Sullivan to Wagner. You also have a will, or rather obstinacy, which will not let you give in, in any argument, however wrong you may be. This being the case, do *you* choose a subject, and *I* will discuss it and be convinced."

"Well," she replied, "seeing that we have known one another about four minutes, I think that is about the coolest speech I ever heard, but at the same time it is marvellously correct. As you don't belong to this place, how did you find all that out?"

"As you took off your gloves, I looked at your hands."

"What *do* you mean?" she asked, and at the same time held up her hands, palms uppermost, as if to see there what had guided us in arriving at a summary of her character, and as she made this motion we continued:—

"I beg to apologize; I was wrong; I see now that we shall get on very well, for you are imaginative (no, not romantic), and so am I, and that you have a painfully keen sense of the ridiculous, which is also my greatest misfortune."

"This is a most extraordinary thing," she returned; "will you tell me how you are analyzing me in this personal but horribly accurate manner?"

"It is quite simple," we said; "with a view to choosing a subject of conversation, I looked at your hands by the light of my favourite science, 'Chirognomy.' By the conical tips of your rather square fingers, and the firmness with which your hand rested on my arm as we came in, I know that you paint.

By the want of method and order shown by your knuckles, joined to the other facts I had remarked, I saw that you were not a deep musician; and, on the top of these, the development of your thumb shows a good-humoured obstinacy; but when you held your palms up to the light, *these* two lines greatly modified and explained my first impressions."

"This interests me very much," said she; "can you tell me my fortune entirely, like a gipsy?"

"Please do not say that," we answered; "fortune-telling is in almost every instance a vulgar swindle practised by charlatans, or worse, for the purpose of extorting money from foolish people. Many professional Chiromants, also, consult the wishes and personal appearance and circumstances of their victims or clients in expounding their pretended knowledge. Amateurs of the science, again, in their desire to be polite, suppress home truths, and the people who present their hands for examination, whilst inwardly thankful that the knowledge evidenced has been so slight, think that the science is simply a masquerade, and its practice a feat of assurance on the part of the practitioner. All these things tend to bring Chiromancy into disrepute; but, nevertheless, the character and disposition of a person is most clearly inscribed in the hand; events, as they happen to us, become written there as with a quill-pen; and as surely as 'coming events cast their shadows before,' so surely are those shadows cast in the hand. You might say, 'The present and the past it may be possible to discern, but the future, no!' I answer: 'Why not? the lines do not become marked in an instant, in the twinkling of an eye; of a line which is destined to appear, the root must necessarily exist somewhere in the hand, and it is the science of Chiromancy which enables us to find those roots and distinguish them from the lines which have already come into prominence.

"You have asked me to read your hand by this science. I warn you of two things: first, that if there is anything in the art (and I, of course, firmly believe that there is), all the secrets of your life are laid bare to my inspection in your hand; second, that whatever I see there I shall tell you without a moment's hesitation, from the most complimentary facts to the most bitter truths; if you have anything to conceal do not show me your hands; if not, and if after these remarks you still elect to submit yourself to this ordeal, give me your hands, and if you repent of it, on your own head be it!"

"Well," she replied, "I consent, I *will* show you my hand; but at the same time this question must now stand adjourned till after dinner. Tell me something about the other people present."

"I can only tell you the outlines of the characters around us. Of course the superficial examination of the external formations of a collection of hands cannot be infallible, but, as far as it can, here goes. That old gentleman over there is hard, calculating, and dictatorial; but if he has any near relations, they find him amiable and tractable *away* from his business, which is mechanical and scientific."

"Very true," replied our neighbour; "he is my uncle, a dear old gentleman, a civil engineer of great experience and some celebrity."

"The lady next to him is a blue-stocking, presumably a spinster, accustomed to command, but underneath kind and sympathetic; the gentleman next her is in business, a clever and clear-headed man; the lady on the other side of him is a pianiste, headstrong and passionate, but the embodiment of good-nature; she is also inquisitive, and nervous. How are we getting on?"

"The first lady you pointed out," was the answer, "is the principal of a girls' school close by; the man in the middle I don't know; the third is my sister, and there you were *quite* right."

The conversation then flowed into other channels, and we did not return to the subject till a few days afterwards when we met at a garden-party in another place, and Miss ——— claimed the fulfilment of the promise; we took her hand, and, with her permission, we recapitulate the most important of the events we saw there.*

"You were born under extraordinary circumstances, and, at the moment of your birth, your life was in danger from some external cause; that is, the danger was not constitutional—you were a strong, healthy baby."

"Very true," replied our victim; "I was born in the Indian Mutiny; my mother was flying from ———, and I was born during the flight."

"Your health has always been generally excellent, though you are subject to headaches; you were, how-

* It should be remarked that the following observations are from the hands of three separate ladies, all somewhat alike in disposition. For convenience sake, and so as not to publish a recognizable portrait, we condense the trio in the subjoined diagnosis.

BOOKS

TAX INVOICE

Sold By:

REKHTA FOUNDATION
Gyan Avenue 12 Pragati Market
Ashok Vihar Phase-II, New Delhi
North West Delhi 110052
Delhi
India
State Code : 07
Ph: 9899492060
GSTIN No.: 07AABTR9771N1ZO

Invoice No. : RMP202048592
Invoice Date : 15/06/2024
Order No. : 46971
Order Date : 15/06/2024

Delivered To:

Mrinal Kumar Sarma
Kali Mandir Path bye lane no.1Borsajai
Parameswar kutir
Kamrup 781040
Assam
India
State Code : 18

Payment Method : cod
Shipped By : Delhivery Surface
AWB No. : 19041592851894
eWaybill No. :

Description	HSN	Qty	Unit Price	Unit Disc.	Taxable Value	IGST	Total
THE LANGUAGE OF THE HAND: Being A Concise Exposition Of the Principles and Practice of the Art of Reading the Hand - Paperback Model : Paperback SKU : 43957694810989		1	306.90	0.00	306.90	0.00	306.90
Shipping Charges					79.00	0.00	79.00
Net Total		1					385.90

Net Amount Payable (In Words):	Three Hundred And Eighty Five Rupees ,nine Paise

All disputes are subject to Delhi jurisdiction only. Goods once sold will only be taken back or exchanged as per the store's exchange/return policy.

Authorised Signature for REKHTA FOUNDATION

Whether tax is payable under reverse charge:No

ever, very ill at five years old, and at nineteen you nearly died of brain-fever."

"Quite right, excepting that my first illness was at six instead of five."

"Once in your life you were nearly drowned. In disposition you are bright and joyous, but if anything goes wrong, you worry over it for a long time instead of making the best of it. You are very self-willed, and act on impulse; it was this that made you crush your first and only love-affair. Please do not correct me—I am certain of it. You have no idea of time. Outwardly you are exceedingly untidy; as a matter of fact, you always know exactly where everything is. You are by no means superstitious, and when I first broached this subject, you thought it interesting but silly, that was impulse; your better reason now tells you that there is a great deal in it. I think all I have said so far is correct."

"I am afraid, and at the same time I am thankful, that it is."

"Your line of fortune is well-marked; your luck is principally derived from your accident on the water somewhere, but though your heart and your common sense are good, your obstinacy and self-will will always be your worst enemies. Your life will be of average length; you will meet with an accident to your head at thirty-five; you will go two long voyages; and when you marry—as you will do—your family will be five in number. On the whole, I congratulate you on your past, present, and future."

The past, which had been brought up to this lady, she admitted was perfectly accurate; the future, as is usual, she refused to believe, but in after years she may see these pages and remember the occasion. She has just left England unexpectedly for ——, and thus the future begins to answer its foreshadowing in her hand.

If the science whose action and results are illustrated by the above citation of facts is merely an amusement, a frivolous charlatanry based on the doctrine of chances, it cannot fail to be pernicious in the extreme, and on that account ought to be put down by the highest authority, as tending towards popular scepticism and superstition; but if, on the other hand, the doctrines which it teaches and the principles which govern it are true, ought it not to receive greater credence and a more widespread indoctrination, for by its means the natural tendencies being discovered, the education may so be directed as to develop those tendencies, instead of crushing them, by a misconceived idea of the direction of the natural talents?

Our fathers would, and did laugh the new-born science to scorn, but the increasing wisdom of generations commences to look upon this and kindred subjects with a less sceptic and more analytical eye. We say the "new-born science," for although the science of Palmistry, in a greater or less state of development, has existed ever since the days of the ancient Egyptians, it is only comparatively recently that the exertions of such men as D'Arpentigny, the Chirognomist, and Desbarolles, the Chiromant, have elevated the Science of the Hand to a position worthy the consideration of learned men.

We consider that the time will come, nay, is not far distant, when all men will be imbued with the importance of this knowledge, for when a large number of men have proved, in their intercourse with their fellow-creatures, the importance and value of the advantage they derive over the rest by an acquaintance with such sciences as Chiromancy, Phrenology, and Physiognomy, the rest, to participate in those advantages, and in self-defence, will also acquire the requisite knowledge, and the affairs of the world will be based not on the *account* a man gives of himself, or gets given of himself by his friends, but by his true character, written in legible characters on his head, his face, and in his hands.

Chirognomy especially is worthy of attention, for whilst it requires the submission of the person to be experimented on to effect a Phrenological or Chiromantic examination, the student of Chirognomy has only to glance at the hands of his neighbour, whether they be occupied or quiescent, to arrive at a complete analysis of the general outlines of his character. Subsequently Chiromancy comes in and tells us the minute events which have passed in a lifetime, that is if the subject will surrender his hand, but the Chirognomist can measure an opponent and analyze a character without the subject of the scrutiny being even aware that he is undergoing an examination, and being read like an open book, as in the opening episode of the narrative which commences this Introduction.

It has often been remarked by men of science and religion, that it is not allowed to presumptuous Man to pry thus into the secrets of the Most High. To them we have always answered, as firm conviction has dictated that an all-seeing Creator has not given us these indications to be passed over and not construed. "In manu omnium Deus signa posuit ut noverint singuli opera sua," says Job (chap. 37, v. 7); but these revelations have not been given us to be dealt with lightly; they have been placed for our instruction and use, but veiled from crass intelligences, that man may by his own efforts take advantage of the powers conferred upon him for his own protection and instruction, and that of those with whom his walk in life is cast.

PART I.

CHIROGNOMY.

PART I.

CHIROGNOMY.

"Manus membrum hominis loquacissimum."

CHAPTER I.

OF THE HAND GENERALLY; AND PARTICULARLY OF THE PALM AND FINGERS.

CHIROGNOMY, understood as distinct from Chiromancy, is the science by which we can tell the dispositions, proclivities, characters, and occupations of those with whom we are thrown in contact, by the mere actual shape of the hands, their outward appearances, and the impressions they give to the senses of vision and touch. D'Arpentigny was the great high priest of this branch of the science (as Desbarrolles was of the other), and he divided all hands into seven categories, as follows:—

1. The Elementary (or Large-palmed).
2. The Necessary (or Spatulate).
3. The Artistic (or Conical).
4. The Useful (or Square)

5. The Philosophical (or Knotty).
6. The Psychic (or Pointed).
7. The Mixed Hand.

If the palm of the hand is too meagre and narrow, it shows a feeble disposition, wanting in versatility or fertility of conception, a nature of weak passions, and without power; if it is supple and of a thickness and size in proportion with the fingers and the rest of the body, it denotes aptitude and brightness of idea; if, though still supple, the mounds and general developments are too marked and gross, it betrays sensuality and egotism; and if at the other extreme it is too big, too fat and gross in itself, it indicates a character void of refinement, and instincts inclining to animality. This delicacy of hand or foot carries itself even to the lower animals, for whilst horses, asses, mules, cows, pigs, and other animals noted for their stupidity have but solid horn feet, the higher animals, and those possessing most instinct, such as the felidæ, dogs, monkeys, and the like, have their feet more or less articulated and delicate as they stand higher or lower in the grade of animal intelligence.

The fingers, again, are smooth, or knotted, and, among the latter, some hands have fingers with two knots, and others with only one. If your second joints (*i.e.*, those nearest the nails) are developed, you have a well-ordered mind; if both joints are developed, this orderliness and method are the more pronounced. With both joints well developed you will be punctual, tidy, systematic, and methodical in your course of action. If you have no knots in your fingers, *i.e.*, if neither joint is developed, your natural tendency will be towards art, and your course of action will be rather inspired than reasoned out; you will be guided by fancy and sentiment rather than knowledge. Good taste (intellectually) belongs to knotted fingers, natural grace to smooth.

The fingers, whether knotted or smooth, have the third phalange (that which bears the nail) either pointed, conical, square, or spatulated. Take two hands both spatulated, but one smooth and the other knotty. Both subjects * will be active, will have an aptitude for physical activity, and an inclination to regard things from their useful, practical side. Both will appreciate things *real*, physical force, calculation, sciences natural, experimental, and physical, and so on. *But* the subject with smooth fingers will succeed in these arts by inspiration, spontaneity, locomotion; whilst the one with jointed or knotty fingers will succeed by calculation, reasoning, and probability.

Now take two other subjects: these have *square* tips to their fingers, but those of the one are smooth, and those of the other jointed. Both, by reason of the square fingers, have tastes for moral sciences, politics social and philosophical, didactic, dramatic and exact poetry, grammar, languages, logic—in fact, the lighter forms of things useful and practical. They prefer that things should be exact and complete than grand and magnificent; they have an aptitude for business, respect of persons, positive but moderate ideas; they like to discover rather than to imagine, to

* By *subject*, we indicate in the following pages the person being operated upon, *i.e.* submitting his or her hand to the Chiromantic examination.

theorize rather than to act on impulse or by calculation. They never attain the most glorious poetic flights, but they excel in literature, sciences, and the more exact arts. The subject with smooth fingers will pursue rather literature, considered *as* literature only, and will pursue his tastes with spontaneity, whilst the one with knotted fingers will proceed as before by calculation and with reason, excelling in history, geography, social science, and the like.

Given: two subjects, one spatulate, the other square, the former will be the more simple but the less polite; he will have greater freedom but less elegance.

Take now a subject having smooth fingers ending conically, or like a thimble. You will find the fine arts, sculpture, vigorous painting, and monumental architecture, imaginative but reasonable poetry, love of the beautiful from its sensible and reasonable point of view, romance, dislike of abstruse calculation, love of independence, enthusiasm sometimes subject to fantasy. If the hand, instead of being smooth, be knotty, you will find the same tendencies, but with more moral force and character.

If knotted fingers have the outer phalange square *and* pointed, they indicate a nature prone to speculative ideas, meditation, and the most philosophical sciences. They indicate love of stern truth, poetry of reason and thought, logic, independence, religious, social, and political, deism, democracy and liberty. This is what we call the philosophic hand, and is more theoretical than practical.

Here is another hand, this time with smooth fingers, and having the third phalange very pointed and drawn out. Here we have ideality, religion, and contemplation in their highest development, indifference to material interests, poetry of soul and heart, desire for love and liberty, adoration of the beautiful in the "hysterical" abstract. We call this the psychic hand, which is absolutely ideal and unpractical.

It will be seen, therefore, that spatulate and square fingers monopolize matter and reality, *i.e.* industries, and useful and necessary arts, action, theory based on *facts*, and intellectual science, whilst conical and pointed fingers indicate—the first; art, by love of the beautiful in its actuality, and the second; the true and beautiful, in their inner significance, and the most ideal and lofty poetry and idealism.

A hand which is hard and stiff, and has a difficulty in opening to its full extension, indicates obstinacy and stubbornness. A large hand indicates love of minutiæ and detail; a medium hand takes in details, but also appreciates entirety. Amongst musical people the most correct and learned musicians have square fingers; instrumentation, whether it be the art of performing, or composing for instruments, is invariably found in spatulate fingers; whilst singers have nearly always the third phalange pointed. Thus it will be understood, that whilst knots beautify and improve a spatulate or square-fingered hand, on account of their natural usefulness and aptitude for combination, to have the joints largely developed would be a deformity and misfortune to a pointed or conical-fingered hand, seeing that the latter are devoted to the finer and more liberal arts, which necessarily succeed best when they are the offspring of inspiration and spontaneity.

The inherent natural shape of a hand never alters.

Its concomitant conditions may be changed by the subject being forced into an occupation the opposite of his genius, inclination, and natural tendency, but the original aptitude, and the form of finger which denotes it, always remain. Thus: If a subject obviously inclined towards, and born for, poetry or art be forced by circumstances to become an engineer, or to pursue any other practical employment, the hand will become hard, gross, and mechanical, but the pointed smooth shape will still remain undisguised.

Take the absolute rustic, free as air, without thought or mental cares of any kind, his hand will be spatulate or square, with large joints. Take the circus-rider, juggler, gymnast, dancer, rider, and so on, his hand will be either spatulate and smooth, or large and conical, and very hard, for these possess a kind of rugged, instinctive grace. Amongst literary men and women the hands will be formed according to the subjects on which, and the styles in which, they write.

It would be easy to pursue this theme, had we time and space for it, *ad infinitum;* but though we might make ourselves clearer on the subject, we should necessarily be obliged to repeat ourselves. An intelligent perusal and comprehension of this chapter will give the reader every necessary information concerning the palm and fingers of the hand, from a general point of view, so that we can now proceed to the consideration of the most important part of the hand, to which we shall devote an entire chapter, and that is THE THUMB.

CHAPTER II.

OF THE THUMB.

"In default of other proofs, the thumb would convince me of the existence of God."—ISAAC NEWTON.

THE Thumb is the most essential part of the human hand, for without it the fingers would be comparatively useless. It is the thumb which constitutes the great difference between the hand of man and the foot of the higher animals; the nearest approach to the human thumb, *i.e.*, the monkey's, is short, and almost immobile, and, therefore, as compared with the human thumb, is almost reduced to the rank of a fifth finger, or nail. The ancient Romans used to denote a coward by the words "pollice truncatus" (a man with his thumb cut off), a term which had its origin in the practice of certain pusillanimous slaves, who used to cut off their thumbs to avoid being sent to the wars, they being considered unfit for anything after suffering this disfigurement; and it is from this phrase that is derived our English word poltroon, through the French *poltron*. In the human thumb lie the indications of his will and intellect; people who are born idiots come into the world either without thumbs or with their thumbs quite abortive and useless. A baby, before it can exercise its will, it will be observed, always keeps its fingers closed over its thumbs, whereas a reasoning man, when exercising his will or determination, almost invariably closes his thumb across his fingers. Epileptic patients during their fits always fold their thumbs inside their hands; indeed, the approach of their fits are often heralded by the preliminary folding of their thumbs; and people at the approach of death almost always hide their thumbs in their hands. At the root of the thumb, says the twin science Chiromancy, (*q.v.* Mount of Venus), lie the indications more or less developed of a tendency to love; and is not love only an exercise of the will, amounting to longing? The first phalange we denominate the phalange of logic, *i.e.*, perception, judgment, and reason, whilst in the second (or outer) phalange we look for the indications of will, invention, decision, and prompt action.

The Romans, again, to return to their recognition of the thumb as an indication of will, used it in their gladiatorial displays, to show, by its erection or depression, their will concerning the defeated combatant. If the second or outer phalange of your thumb be narrow, mean, and short, your will is a weak one; you are prone to accept received notions, to be guided by others; you are doubtful, uncertain, and indifferent. People whose thumbs are small are more sentimental than others whose thumbs are in proportion, or large, and they act more on impulse than reflexion; those whose thumbs are large have consequently exactly opposite characteristics. A large thumb usually indicates independence, a tendency towards despotism, presence of power, but power born of force, not of charm. Following these reasonings you will find that persons with a taste for the occult sciences have large thumbs.

Any one who has smooth fingers and a small thumb

has (whatever may be the form of the third phalange of his fingers) an inborn tendency to poetry and art, though he may not have the talent to cultivate them. We know an eminent literary man whose ideas in general are of the most matter-of-fact description, who sits wrapt and spell-bound at hearing beautiful music or poetry, though he has not the least talent for either of these arts; his fingers are smooth, but spatulate with small thumbs. Subjects with conical or pointed fingers and large thumbs temper their idealism and art by deduction and reason; in fact, their temperament resembles that of subjects with square-fingers, but a small thumb.

Carrying, therefore, your mind back to what we said concerning the characteristics indicated by the forms of the fingers, you will arrive at this deduction, that the subject with smooth, conical, or pointed fingers will have the characteristics of that form the more strongly developed if he has also a small thumb, whilst the subject with knotted fingers, terminating squarely or in spatule, will be the more powerfully addicted to the tendencies of that form, if to them he adds a thumb which is large. Thus by their nature people with large thumbs can produce results unnatural to them more easily than those with small; for example, a large-thumbed mechanican may bring himself to write poetry, but a small-thumbed poet can never become a practical calculator

CHAPTER III.

OF THE CONSISTENCY OF HANDS.

By consistency, we mean the impression produced by a hand upon the sense of touch. Thus two hands may be of the same size and shape, the fingers of both formed and terminating in the same manner, but with this difference; that one hand is soft and supple, whilst the other is firm, almost to hardness. Take two hands with spatulate fingers possessing this difference; they both have the tendency towards action, but the soft hand will affect a temperate movement and activity, whilst the hard-handed subject will tend towards energy and powerful action. The soft-handed subject will be active, but take his full share of sleep, whilst the hard-handed one will rise with the lark to be up and doing. Take two artists in the same way; the hard-handed one will execute works showing manly occupations and phases of life; he of the soft hands will be less practical in his subjects, but more diverse, more proneto ideas of the moment and fancy, and possess more delicacy. People with soft hands always have the little fleshy ball on the face of the outer phalanges more developed, and this seems to give them better taste and tact. People with hard hands are seldom, if ever, polished and gentle in manner, but they are often good-natured and sensitive; those with fat, soft hands are usually indolent, luxurious, and of stagnant intellect. As we grow old and careworn, our hands, as a rule, become hard, or, at least, firm-skinned and stiff. This is accounted for by the fact that our imagination fades, our sense of the poetic and beautiful becomes less keen, and from artistic and imaginative amusements we turn to tastes for arrangement of house and home, gardening and the like; and it is particularly noticeable, and always has been, that in numberless instances men with great intellects have, as their minds have faded, been taken with a love of manual labour, which shows itself in gardening particularly, the hands becoming parchmenty and ossified, apart from the question of natural decay; in the same way, as with age, our joints become more prominent, we get less open to impressions, less credulous, and more argumentative and logical.

Subjects with hard hands are capable of true and ardent love, though they are seldom capable of much tenderness; smooth-handed people, on the other hand, are more capable of tenderness and affection than deep love. The beau ideal of a hand is that which is firm without being hard, and supple without being soft, such hands as this betoken a liberal intelligence and active mind, such subjects combine theory and practice; and however much they may work with their fingers their hands hardly ever harden, and then only very slowly, whereas hands already very firm have a great tendency to become very hard. According, therefore, to their temperament (shown in the *consistency* of their hands) people cultivate the talents and tendencies to which the formation of their fingers and hands generally incline them.

A large, soft hand with spatulated fingers evidences

a love of action, but not of its own activity. Such a subject enjoys looking on at reviews, at athletics, and at games of skill without taking part in them; he likes to read books of travels and adventures, but does not embark upon them himself.

Thus, therefore, it will be seen that though the forms of the hand betoken certain tastes and characteristics, we must look to the consistency of the hand to see how those tastes are cultivated, and how those characteristics develop themselves. Having now discussed the characteristics of various hands, we will proceed to consider the seven types which, following D'Arpentigny, we set down categorically at the beginning of these chapters on Chirognomy.

CHAPTER IV.

OF THE SEVEN TYPES OF HANDS.

I. The Elementary Hand (Fig. 1). — The characteristics of this hand are thick, stiff fingers, a short thumb, generally turned back, large, broad, and thick palm, very hard. Such is the hand of the labourer, the stableman, the soldier who fights only for fighting's sake, the colonist who merely exists in a foreign clime by the sweat of his brow. Such subjects understand nothing but the grossly material aspect of things; they are inaccessible to reason, their virtues are negative, they conform to rules from

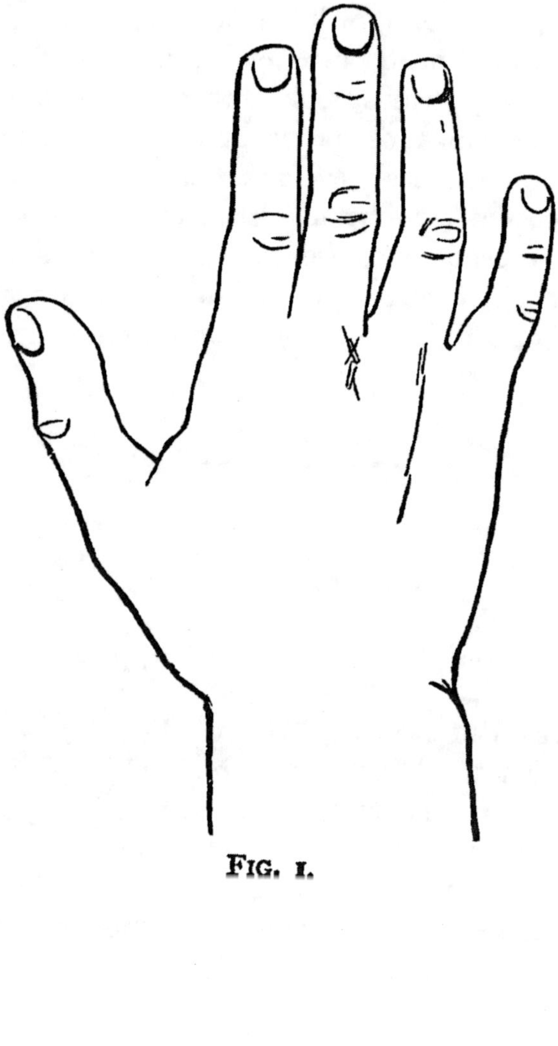

FIG. 1.

sheer want of originality. Such a hand betrays heaviness of soul, sluggish imagination, and complete indifference. The Laplanders are almost without exception of this type; amongst the warm, intelligent, poetic East Indians this type is practically unknown. As a matter of fact, in warm latitudes (such as ours) the hand absolutely elementary is exceedingly rare, excepting among the Tartars and Sclavs, whose instincts and ferocity are merely brutal. The subject with elementary hands is subject to superstitions more or less poetic, according as the fingers are more or less conic; and they, of all other types, succumb most readily to griefs and disappointments, being utterly void of resources.

II. THE SPATULATE HAND (Fig. 2).—First take a spatulate hand with a big thumb. This subject is resolute rather than resigned, and is always ready to take measures to avert the ills which flesh is heir to, of which measures the conic hand knows nothing. He has great confidence in himself, and there is this great difference between the Elementary and the Spatulate Hand—the former seeks only the necessary, the latter desires and strives after abundance. The spatulate subject possesses the instinct of self-preservation highly developed, and he rules the world of *things material* by natural intelligence and material instinct. Such a subject, having senses more active than delicate, finds it easier to be constant and faithful in love than it is for souls inclined to poesie: he is, in fact, more amenable to duty and custom than sensitive to the charms of youth and beauty. Fingers smooth, but spatulate indicate an appreciation for elegance as well as comfort; but an appreciation of fashionable rather than artistic elegance. Such hands are commoner in Scotland than in England, in England than in France, and in France than in Spain, as also they are commoner in mountainous than in plane countries. People with spatulated fingers make excellent colonists, for they are not rendered flighty by tastes for poetry and art; they only become attached to the ground on account of its products; they love manual labour and action of all kinds; they suffer unless they have abundance, but do not seek after superfluous advantages, for they are only very moderately sensual, and are more prone to be greedy than epicurean. Their love of locomotion reconciles them to their self-imposed exile, ready for all events, and accustomed to count on themselves; they have no objection to solitude, and they are clever at all physical sciences, attaching themselves in life only to those things that are immovable and constant.

The spatulate fingered subject admires architecture for its quantity rather than its quality, preferring the immense to the beautiful. He likes to be astonished, and to contemplate works which make him think of the immense amount of physical labour which must have been employed to construct them. The artist is sunk in the artisan, opulence predominates over luxury; wherever this type is found, *i.e.*, the large hand with spatulate fingers and a large thumb, these same predilections will be the guiding rule of that subject's life, the useful rather than the ornamental, the necessary rather than the superfluous, the actual rather than the ideal. If the thumb be small their active physical instincts will be more unrestrained but

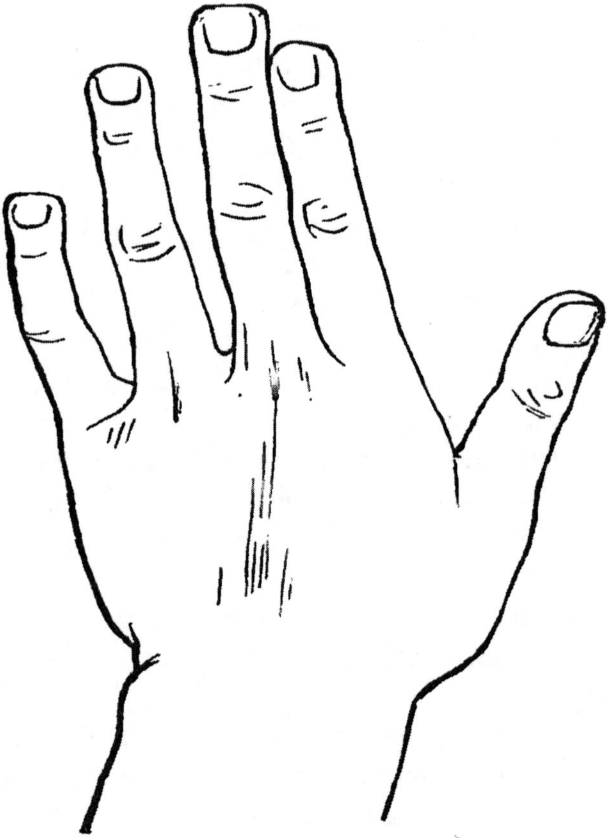

FIG. 2.

less pronounced and forcible, partaking more of the nature of the square hand (*q.v.*).

III. THE ARTISTIC HAND (Fig. 3). — This hand has three tendencies, which are very different to one another, but only marked by slight distinctions in the hand itself. These are:—(i.) A supple hand and a small thumb with a medium palm indicating love of beauty, and particularly of form. (ii.) Large, short, and thick with a large thumb betrays a desire for riches, fortune, and greatness. (iii.) Large and very firm hands mean a tendency to sensuality. All three are governed by inspiration, and are ill-adapted to the mechanical arts. The first is actuated by enthusiasm, the second by stratagem and scheme, and the third by the suggestion of pleasure. Barring these differences of characteristic, the tendencies of these hands are the same, though the most characteristic is that which has the fingers large at the first phalange and narrowing to a more or less obtuse cone. The thumb is small and the palm is moderately developed. Such a subject will attach himself, by instinct and without consideration, to the beautiful aspect of ideas and things; he will prefer the ornamental to the useful without much regard for reality, greedy of leisure, novelty, and liberty; at the same time ardent and timid, humble and vain, he is energetic and impulsive rather than powerful or forcible; his spirits are apt to plunge from ecstasy to despair, unable to command, but incapable of obedience; he is *attracted* rather than led by duty. He is enthusiastic and cannot put up with the restraints of regular, and what we might call, domestic life; his thoughts are sentiments rather than ideas; light-hearted and original he has generally a warm imagination, but a cold heart. Such a combination of unrestrained instincts of pleasure and want of moral stamina is therefore the character of artists in general, or, at any rate, those who live only for their art. They only have to like a thing to adore it; they submit, as a rule, to faith and orthodoxy because thus they are saved the trouble of reasoning; but they are intolerant of political despotism, because of the actual restraints it places upon them. This love of art is the first emotion to which an uncultivated mind is amenable; a love of form and beauty often exists among savage tribes who are wanting in the utter rudiments of civilization, and for this reason it is the most engrossing and powerful of all human tendencies; races who are too lazy to cultivate any other taste cling tenaciously to and highly develop this one; it is thus that among the ignorant artistic peasantry of Southern Europe that this type of hand, modifying the elementary type, is so largely prevalent. It is among people possessing these hands that we often find subjects possessing only the *evil* propensities of their type, sensuality, laziness, egotism, singularity, cynicism, love of dissipation, intellectual incapacity, sharpness, and tendency to falsehood and exaggeration. Love, which is not a matter of the senses, such as filial, fraternal, and paternal affection, is rare among hands of this class, and belongs principally to square and spatulate hands.

IV. THE USEFUL HAND (Fig. 4) is of medium size, but inclining to large, the joints of the fingers developed, and the outer phalange square, the thumb large, and developed at the root, the palm of medium

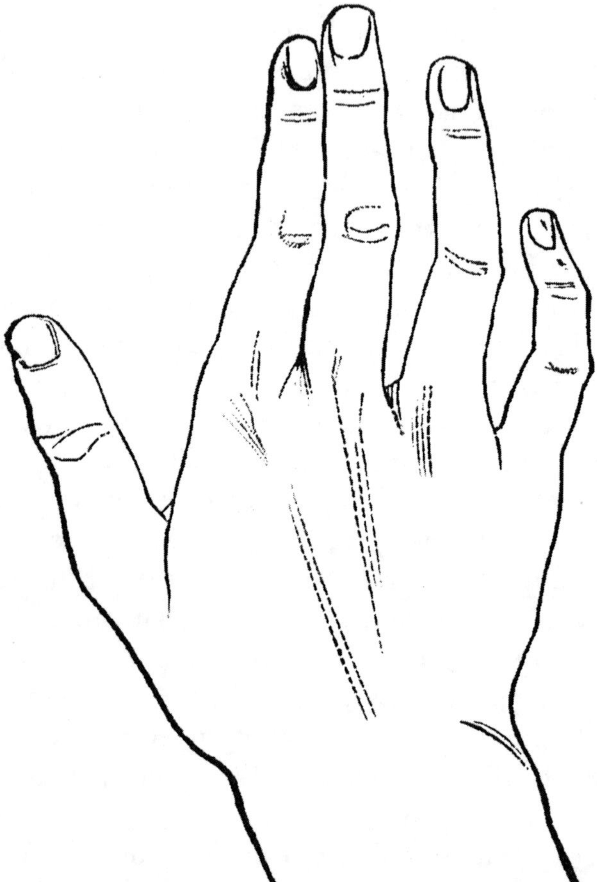

FIG. 3.

size, hollowed and firm. Perseverance, foresight, order, and submission to rule, all qualities conspicuous by their absence in the artistic hand, are particularly the characteristics of the useful hand, *i.e.*, that hand whose leading feature is the square tips of its fingers. To organize, classify, and regulate is their province; with them the beautiful and true are subordinate to theory and rule; they have a strong love of similitude and uniformity as opposed to the change and contrast, which is the delight of the conical-fingered hand; they appreciate the differences in things apparently similar and the points of resemblance in things outwardly dissimilar. They are apt to confuse discipline and civilization, compulsory order and the order of common consent; they only act on the promptings of sense and reason, and are consequently often somewhat narrow-minded. They are polite and courteous by reason of their respect of persons and their sense of order and the fitness of things; their literature is precise and careful, their poetry rythmic and complete, in language they use terms more generic than distinctive, *i.e.*, they will say "dog" rather than "mastiff," "terrier," "beagle," or as the case may be; "ship" rather than "frigate," "man-o'-war," "brig," and so on. Their books are and must be clear and correct in their expositions, leaving nothing to the imagination, and being well arranged and indexed. Cautious and far-seeing, they like what is known, but suspect what is undefined; their ideas being moderate they prefer the real to the apparently real; they incline to men of good sense more than to men of genius, and are more noted for spirit and talent than for imaginative faculties; their moral axioms are that the good is better than the beautiful, and the useful is better than both. These qualities are apt to become despotic in the hold they have over these subjects, leading them into hypocrisy, which is the result of morbid love of reserve, regularity of conduct, and personal respect, coldness which they mistake for moderation, flattery and adulation to which they are peculiarly susceptible, stiffness of manner, unbending punctuality, and steady but suppressed ambition. For his friends such a subject chooses men cultivated, disciplined, and, so to speak, modelled on a correct pattern.

Such subjects prefer privilege to liberty; they are prepared to submit to the authority of rank, birth, law and custom, and they like to feel and make others feel the check-string. The man with large square hands is always neat, well brushed and buttoned up, or else carefully *négligé;* he is regular in his meals, and does not eat at odd hours; his mind will be just and equally balanced, but he will not be brilliant. There is this difference between the spatulate and the square hand. Both like and respect authority, but the former will be fond of the ruler individually, whilst the latter admires and respects the institution of authority itself. The artistic hand only admires regularity when it is subservient to, and a component part of, a beautiful whole; the useful hand only admires the beautiful when that beauty is the result of regularity. Thus, therefore, it will be seen that though the useful hand is the most desirable, from a worldly point of view, it is neither so happy as the artistic, nor so conscientious and independent as the spatulate, but it is the square fingers

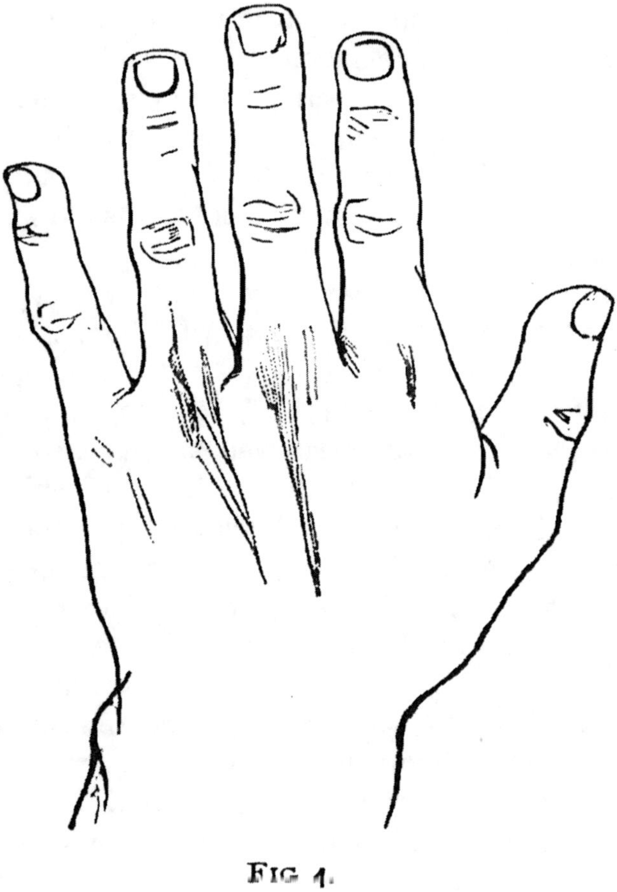

FIG 1.

of the useful hand which govern almost the entire world.

V. The Philosophic Hand (Fig. 5).—Palm medium size and pliable, the fingers knotted, and the third phalange an obtuse cone verging on the square, having a sort of oval, clubbed appearance, consequent on the development of the second joint, the thumb large, having its two phalanges of equal length, indicating an equal share of will and logic. The distinguishing characteristic of this particular form of exterior phalange or finger-tip, semi-square and semi-conical, is an innate tendency to search after, a love for, the absolute truth and reality of things. The developed joints of the philosophic hand give it calculation, deduction and method, the semi-conical shape of the fingers indicates an intuition of poetic instinct. Such a subject prefers reality to beauty, and cause rather than effect; is gifted with an enthusiasm for moral, experimental and philosophic sciences; has a leaning towards analysis, *i.e.*, he likes to sound the meaning and cause of his sensations and ideas, the problems of creation and the origin of things; he does not hold his opinions, belief and ideas at second-hand, but only after having turned them over, viewed them from all sides, and examined them thoroughly. He is governed by reason rather than by faith or love, sacrificing to reason all such minor considerations as custom and fashion; this guiding influence imbues him with a love of ethics, and political and social economy, often leading him to scepticism and heresy, but never to fanaticism. He is open to doubt, but does not object to being so; he considers things in detail, and also in mass; individuals and also communities; he studies both the rule and its exceptions; the order, which is an inherent quality in him, shows itself in classifying rather than in arranging, *i.e.*, he will separate things according to to their character and nature rather than by their size and appearance; he pays no attention to vain scruples, superstitious terrors, and is moderate in his pleasures. Thus it will be seen that reason is the principal characteristic of this hand; it will take nothing on trust; at the same time there is a refinement, an appreciation of the beautiful, indicated by the semi-conic formation of the fingers. It has the actuality and truth of the spatulate hand without its stubbornness and lack of refinement; it has the analysis of the square hand without its insincerity, and the refinement of the conic hand without its flightiness and selfishness. Its motto is "Moderation in all things, and truth in all."

VI. THE PSYCHIC HAND (Fig. 6).—This is the rarest and most beautiful hand of all. In proportion to the formation of the subject whose it is, it is small; the palm is of medium size, the fingers without knots, the third phalange long and pointed the thumb small and well shaped. If the hand i large and the joints are developed, it has more force than is usual, but not so much originality. Such subjects are guided by the ideal, by the sublime, and by the soul. They worship at the shrine of beauty and imagination, and are the exact opposite of the philosophical-handed subject. Such subjects never become rulers or statesmen; their idealism and love of the beautiful unreal raises them above such ambition; in strife they disdain small achievements, em-

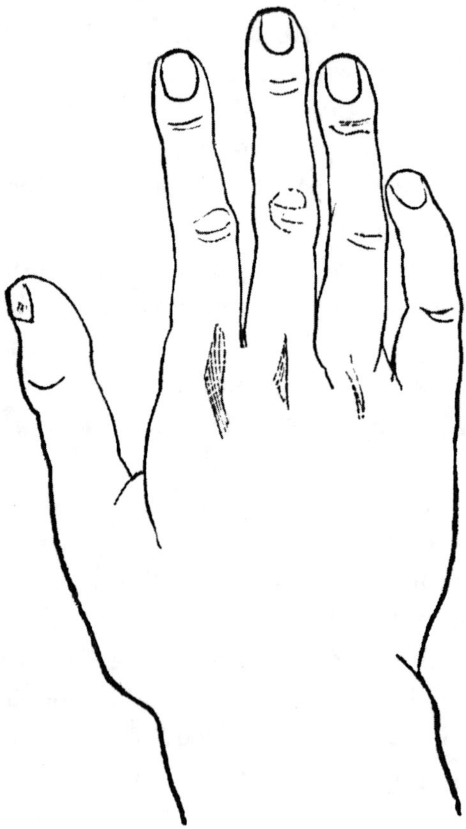

FIG. 5.

barking enthusiastically on the most forlorn nopes, spurred to victories by their fervour of soul and not by their activity of body. Some writers have claimed these hands as the exclusive inheritance of the nobly born. This is a great and incomprehensible mistake; for though it is always rare, it is found among all classes, sometimes among the lowest, where it is crushed and disdained, by reason of its inability to force itself to manual labour. Artistic hands seek imagination and art everywhere, useful hands seek arrangement and rule, philosophic hands seek human reason; to psychic hands is reserved the privilege of a search after ethical divine reason in its highest development; theirs is the faculty for striving after purity and right in the abstract, apart from any questions of convenience. It would be easy to rhapsodize over the advantages, the psychical æsthetic advantages, of this type; but alas! beautiful as it is, innately grand as it is, its impracticability keeps it back in the great race of life. Beautiful in itself it refines us, us of the more worldly types, but without us it could not live. Such natures we must work to support for the privilege of having them amongst us!

VII. The Mixed Hand (Fig. 7).—This is the name of a rather common and rather confusing type, and is the name we give to a hand when, by the confusion of the forms represented in it, it seems to belong to two different types. Thus, for instance, if in a spatulate hand the type is so slightly marked as to be easily mistaken for a square hand; or an elementary conic hand which may be mistaken for an artistic hand; or a highly developed artistic hand which may be mistaken for a psychic hand; a philosophic for a useful and so on, and in all cases *vice versâ*. Such hands partake of the nature of both types represented, or quasi-represented. It is to such hands as these that we must look for intelligence in mixed works, intermediate ideas and sciences, which require more than mere science to elucidate them; such as administration, the theory of commerce, arts which may be called unpoetic, the beauty and actuality of industry and labour, and the art of making the best of, and most out of, everything. Such hands generally indicate that the subject is (as our proverb puts it) "Jack-of-all-trades, master of none;" *i.e.*, they are handy and clever at innumerable pursuits, but they seldom excel greatly in any one; as I have said just above, their capacity for "making the best of it" and their general moral indifference standing in the way of excellence in any one line. They have this great difference from subjects whose hands are of a particular type; these last have talents more pronounced than versatile; people whose hands are mixed are more versatile than individual. The former are instructive to talk to, the latter amusing; the latter succeed best when their most pronounced talent is assiduously cultivated, in which case they succeed enormously.

Take, for instance, the example we have given in Fig. 7. This is what we might call the artistico-elementary hand. This ugly-looking hand, less supple and more thick than the true artistic hand, has not, however, the largeness, the grossness and extreme hardness of the true elementary hand. The fingers are big, smooth (sometimes with one joint swollen; not *developed*, but *swollen*), the thumb

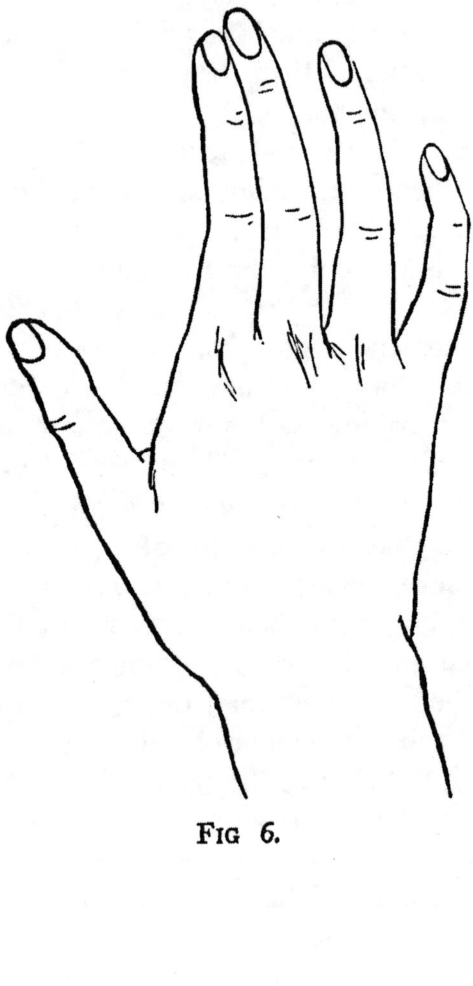

FIG 6.

big, and the general character of the hand conical. Such a subject is greedy but avaricious, *i.e.*, he is sensual, but he only gratifies his sensuality when he can do so at a small expense; he is moral, but without principle; he keeps the law, but is not ethically just; he is sanctimonious, perchance bigoted, without being pious; though he is hardy he will not endure hardships which bring him no corresponding advantage. Such a hand closes easily, but opens with difficulty; this is the case, metaphorically as well as actually; it is not apt at hard work, or manual labour, but it excels at scheming, arranging and negotiating for its own advantage, the manual labours of others.

Other varieties of the mixed hand it would be easy to enumerate, had we space and time; and did we not think that the dissertations we have already given on the various types will enable the reader easily to decipher, or imagine such for himself, such would be the psychico-elementary hand, whose characteristics would be a high intelligence and love of art, but an ignorant indifference to things real, and so on; but in all cases what virtues or good qualities they possess are traceable, so to speak, to an intellectual torpor.

Thus far have we deemed it necessary to consider and discuss the sister science of Chirognomy before proceeding to the consideration of the actual science of Chiromancy. It is most important to be well grounded in Chirognomy before studying Chiromancy, and for obvious reasons. Before you can tell a man his instincts, habits of life, his past, his present and his probable future, it is of the highest importance that you should have a clear insight into his character and tendencies; and, again, as we have said in our introduction (*q.v.*), Chirognomy may be practised without the subject being a consenting party, whilst Chiromancy necessitates, at the least, a close examination of the hand. Before, however, proceeding on our way, we shall pause a few moments to make a few remarks, which seem to us to be necessary, on the subject of SEX.

CHAPTER V.

OF THE FEMALE HAND.

THE characteristics of each type, as we have enumerated them, apply to women as well as to men, though we have, for convenience sake, made use throughout of the masculine pronoun; at the same time, there are certain modifications which seem to require exposition; as, for instance, the square spatulate types are much less pronounced in woman than in man, a fact shown by the greater suppleness and elasticity of the female hand in general, consequent on the differences existing between the male and female dispositions. The man creates, but the woman develops; to man belongs the faculty of principle, to woman the gift of form; our laws are made by man, but our morals by woman; and it has been justly said that man is the spirit of the woman, but woman

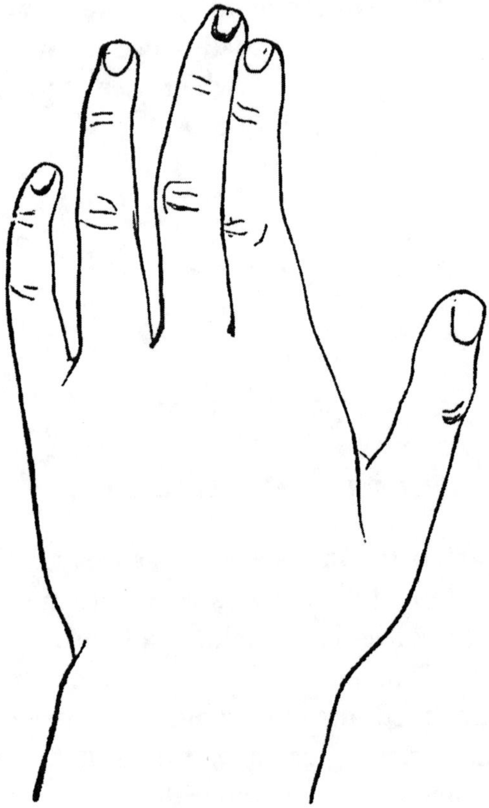

FIG. 7.

is the soul of the man. Few women have their joints developed, so few women have the faculty of combination; in intellectual occupations they choose generally those requiring more tact than science, more activity of mind than of body, more imagination than judgment; if their hands are knotty, their intellects are, so to speak, diluted; they are then less impressionable, and less given to the inspirations of fancy. Women may be divided by this our science into two classes: those with large and those with small thumbs; the first, more intelligent than sensitive, have a natural taste for history and similar studies; the second, more sensitive than intellectual, prefer romance. Consideration and clear headedness is the gift of those with large thumbs; love with them is more a matter of head than heart, but it is also more free and faithful, and a large-thumbed woman is never a coquette. With those who have a small thumb, on the contrary, love is their all in all, and though they are not so clever, they are infinitely more fascinating. The cares of womanhood, the sympathy which is natural to her, and the troubles of maternity, all require and enforce a high degree of intelligence; therefore the elementary hand is of extremely rare occurrence among women; and in communities where the men represent for the most part this type the empire of woman is supreme. Man under these circumstances is dead to the charms of youth, and nearly always marries a woman older than himself, to be governed by her.

English women usually have the exterior phalange delicately squared, consequent on their willingness to adopt household cares. The women of the Oriental harems, on the other hand, devoted unto death, have, generally, small slim hands, with small thumbs. Such wómen as Charlotte Corday, Sophie de Condorcet, and Lucile Desmoulins, women whose very souls were permeated only with one feverish ideal, had very pointed fingers. Take a woman with rather spatulate fingers and a small thumb; such a woman has an unlimited fund of affection and freedom of soul, love of activity, and knowledge of real life; she loves and understands horses, and all other animals; her ideas are practical and useful. The woman with square fingers and a small thumb will have everything in her house orderly and punctual, but without tyranny or despotism; by her example she keeps all things neat and under control. If she have a large thumb, it indicates a virago, tyrannical towards her servants and towards her children; at the same time, the square phalange may indicate narrow-mindedness, prudishness, and fussiness if the hand inclines to hardness. Little, soft, supple hands, with marked joints, and a pretty colour, indicate sharpness, vivacity and brilliancy; love with them must be gay, for their sole object is to be merry. If a woman have hands with a strong palm, conic fingers, and a small thumb, they are most accessible to rhetoric and the fervid language of love, which explains, palliates, extols all things; to please them you must be brilliant, for they prefer oratory and persuasion to logic and sound sense. Delicate, smooth-pointed fingers, with a little thumb and a narrow elastic palm, proclaim an indolent enthusiasm; such women are governed more by heart than by sense and spirit; they do not care about the realities of life and conventional duties; they are pious, but hardly devoted; enthusiastic in spirit, but not in body.

Thus, it will be seen that, though the types have much the same characteristics among women as among men, yet, to read the character of a woman, as shown by her hand, requires more tact and self-confidence than is required in reading that of a man. But, without multiplying instances, we hope that the notes contained in this chapter may aid the would-be Chiromant to analyse and discern these differences; and having shortly enumerated the points of importance to be remembered with regard to Chirognomy, we may safely launch the reader upon the more tempestuous and dangerous sea of Chiromancy.

PART II.

CHIROMANCY.

PART II.

CHIROMANCY.

"Chiromancy hath these aphorisms to foretell melancholy."
—BURTON.

CHAPTER I.

OF THE HAND AND ITS MARKINGS.

ALL hands have lines inscribed upon them. Let any number of individuals assemble, and if they inspect their palms, or have impressions taken of them, they will not find two pairs of hands exactly alike in many thousands of individuals. The right and left hands may be, and are frequently, almost similar in the same person, though as a general rule the right hand possesses dissimilarities which correct and control the indications of the left, and *vice versâ;* but the hands of any two individuals will vary as much as their other features.

There are certain conditions to be observed by any one who wishes to examine the hand of a friend, with a view to reading his disposition or probable future. For instance, the hands examined should be perfectly clean. They should not be inspected immediately after a full meal, or after strong exercise, for then they will appear heated, and the lines will appear more reddened than is natural. For the same reason they should not be in summer too warm, nor, for a different reason, too cold in winter; for, in the latter case, the natural heat being extracted, a paleness is noticeable, which would not under normal conditions exist. Wine and good food excite the body, and naturally influence the palms of the hands.

Besides these very obvious precautions, others should be observed with reference to the sex, age, and constitution of the person who is under inspection. These conditions being observed by a skilful practitioner, he will be enabled to make a very excellent report upon the past, present, and future of the subject under examination; a report which, however unpalatable to the listener, or however agreeable to his vanity, will be absolutely true in all essential particulars. The hand has been compared, and rightly compared, to a looking-glass, and we can see ourselves as others see us—or do *not* see us, as we may perhaps, thankfully remember.

Later on we will give a few instructions for the mode of proceeding. Just now we will quote a celebrated Chiromant, whose claims are by no means exaggerated. He says:—

"Give me the hand of an artist of talent, and without ever having seen his pictures, I will tell him whether he prefers form or colour; if he cares for details, or is satisfied with the massive; whether he works by reflection, or by inspiration; whether he prefers the imitation of nature, or works of imagination. . . . . I will predict for him a greater or less degree of success, or a greater or less degree of fame. . . . . I will tell a physician how he treats his patients, what is his method of ascertaining a disease, whether by inspiration or reflection, or by tracing events to their cause."

This, perhaps, may appear to some an impossibility, but such a knowledge of mankind is within the reach of all who will carefully study the science, which we cannot *fully* unfold within the limits of this little volume. But sufficient will be found for all ordinary purposes of general Chiromancy; and the reader may, in a reasonable time, and with a good memory, read, mark, and learn from many hands the events of many lives, and the disposition of his relatives and friends, as well as his own chances. Modern Chiromants will not pay much attention to the conditions we have enumerated, and so they may make mistakes, *and nothing in the whole world is easier than to err in reading a hand when the reader is inexperienced!* Now for a few hints.

Let the hand be gently contracted, not held out flat, the muscles relaxed so that the hand is as "flabby" as possible. The left hand is first inspected, then compared with the right. The colour of the hand is important. Paleness is not always a good sign. "It denoteth an evil temperament" in those lines which look otherwise coloured, for "redness in some lines signifies evil, and paleness good" (Old tradition.)

Strongly-marked lines in a female hand are held generally to indicate a virago.

The hands must be considered as to quantity and their proportions to the body, and whether they be longer or shorter than they ought to be. The fingers also must have attention; for instance, a long palm with gross fingers denotes a dull and heavy person. Long slender hands denote a tyrannical disposition, and, according to some old authorities, the amount of hair upon the back of them is significant of a good temperament or of an unstable one, according as the hirsuteness be less or more. (*Vide supra* "Chirognomy," Ch. I.)

The parts of the hand for our investigation are divided, and when it is extended open we find the *Vola*, or inner part of the hand, where the lines are; *Tubercula*, or rising parts; the *Ferriens*, or smiting part*; the *Cavea*, or hollow; and the *Mensa*, or table. The five fingers, viz., the *Pollex* or thumb, the *Index* or fore-finger, the *Medius* or middle finger, the *Annularius* or ring finger, and the *Auricularis* or little finger, have each a bearing on the question. In fine, the elements to be considered are the thumb, fingers, joints, lines, and the rising parts, or mountains of the hand.

OF THE PALM OF THE HAND.

Before proceeding to explain the mounds of the hand we will make a few observations concerning the division of the palm, and the curious deductions

* Called also the "Percussion."

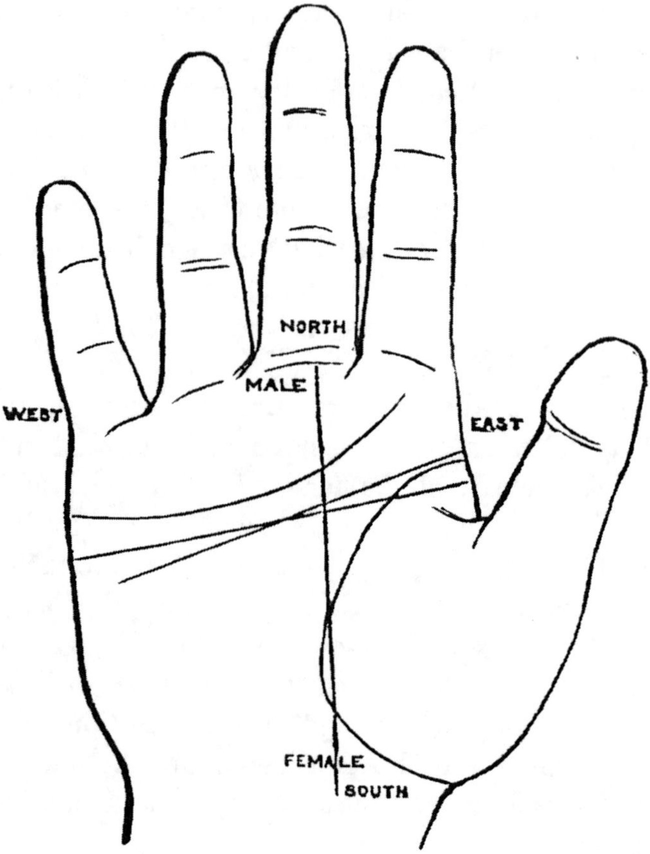

FIG. 8.

which writers have made from it. We shall soon see that the hand is divided into three zones or parts, which are bounded by certain lines to be hereafter explained.

Our readers will perceive, when they consider the qualities attributed to certain mounts, that the upper or northern divisions of the hand contain all the manly, aggressive and hardy qualities. The male portion or the upper part (*Vide* Fig. 8) have industry in Mercury; art based on sciences in Apollo; ambition and force in Jupiter; in the three first fingers, or rather in their bases. Mark this and continue.

Let us look now at the southern or female side—the lower portion of the hand. Here we have sensuality, imagination, love, and various feminine attributes as distinguished from hardiness and aggressiveness. This is evident.

Now compare the inhabitants of the North and South countries of the world. Do we not find the hardy Norseman and the sensuous Southerner, the working, energetic Northerner, and the siesta-loving Southerner? In the one case we have the worker, in the other the *dilettante*, the manly qualities as a rule in one, the feminine or easy-going attributes in the other. This is, at any rate, a curious coincidence, and is really no coincidence. It is nature—Providence—what you will. The fact remains; and the hand of man is held up in the great concourse of the world to confirm the testimony of the Creator—nothing is in vain.

It is scarcely necessary to pursue this particular portion of the subject farther. M. Desbarrolles, in his exhaustive treatise upon the "Mysteries of the

Hand," gives reasons for assigning also the terms east and west to the two sides of the hand, and argues from Europe to America. We will not follow him across the Atlantic to what he terms the "home of Egotism;" and "Egotism is the death of Art." He looks upon the Western Continent apparently as a kind of Moon which is illuminated by the Sun of the East, but when once the Sun disappears the Moon will cease to shine; it has no light of its own. "The future is not in the West; the end is there." He winds up somewhat bitterly—

"On a dit 'la jeune Amerique'!"

"Où est sa jeunesse? Où est sa naïveté, son élan, sa tendresse? Qu'a-t-elle de jeune? Elle a pris tout d'un coup les cheveux blancs de civilization; la corruption. Elle a tous les vices du vieillard sceptique et desséché, et elle aspire à commander le monde. Allons donc! C'est la tête qui commande, parfois c'est le cœur, mais ce n'est jamais le bras!"

The chief points of the hand being now, we hope, understood, we will proceed to examine the "Mounts" and the "Lines" in their order.

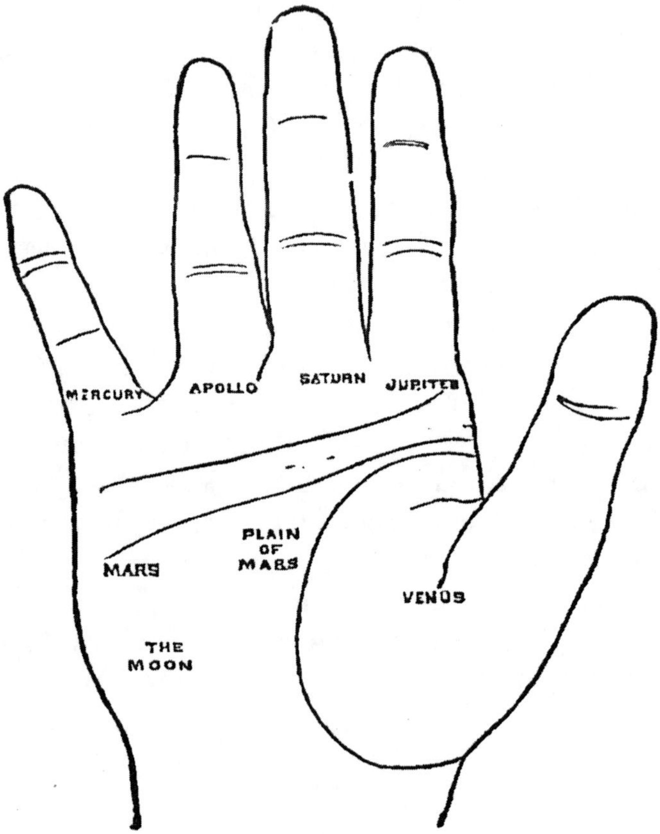
MERCURY
APOLLO
SATURN
JUPITER
PLAIN OF MARS
MARS
VENUS
THE MOON

FIG. 9.

CHAPTER II.

THE MOUNDS OF THE HAND.

THE most casual observer of his hand will notice that at the base of each finger in the palm of the hand is a mound or rising, or a depression. (*Vide* Fig. 9.) Each of these corresponds to a planet, and the star may be fortunate or unfortunate according to its development, and to the corresponding influences of the lines and marks or signs.* The thumb is most important; round its mount runs the line of life; the thumb in Chiromancy is the life, and its influence may be benefited or counteracted by the other little hills which the hand is heir to. The mount of the thumb is sacred to *Venus*. (*Vide supra*, "Chirognomy," Ch. II.)

The mounts beneath the four fingers are—commencing with the Index—*Jupiter*, *Saturn*, *Apollo* (the Sun), *Mercury*. The Mount of *Mars* is at the side of the hand opposite the thumb, immediately below the Mount of Mercury. The Mount of the *Moon* is beneath Mars at the base of the hand opposite the Mount of Venus. We may again observe that the upper or north of the hand is *Male*, the lower portion, near the wrist, the southern or female part. The accompanying diagram and the

* We use the customary planetary terms, because they serve to elucidate our meaning, and distinguish different characteristics, but it must not be supposed that we mix astrology and such-like charlatanism with our Science.

frontispiece will assist our readers in determining the various positions of the mounds.

It may be accepted that when the various hills are properly placed in the positions indicated, they argue the possession of the qualities belonging to each planet. For instance, Jupiter indicates pride, Saturn fatality, Apollo art or riches, Mercury science or wit, Mars self-restraint or perhaps cruelty, the Moon folly or imagination, Venus, love, even to excess and ill-regulated passion.

We must also understand that when these mounds are very slight, their absence indicates the want of the quality in question—a cavity means that a corresponding fault is inherent, while a great excess is equally a defect unless counteracted by the influence of the lines. Perhaps a classification of the various qualities of the mounts and their possible meanings will be more intelligible than a long explanation. Let us commence with the Thumb, the seat of affection. "C'est l'amour qui fait tourner le monde."

THE MOUNT OF VENUS is at the root of the thumb. The line of Life encircles it as a river flows beneath a mountain. "Life is dependent on Love." The presence of the mount supposes grace, beauty, melody in music, dancing, a desire to please, tenderness, politeness, and kindred social virtues which attract the opposite sex. *The absence of the Mount* does not necessarily indicate vice, but it argues want of energy, selfishness, coldness, and want of soul generally. *In excess* it portends vanity, license idleness, faithlessness, coquetry, &c., to an extent commensurate with the abnormal development, if unchecked by religion and good sense.

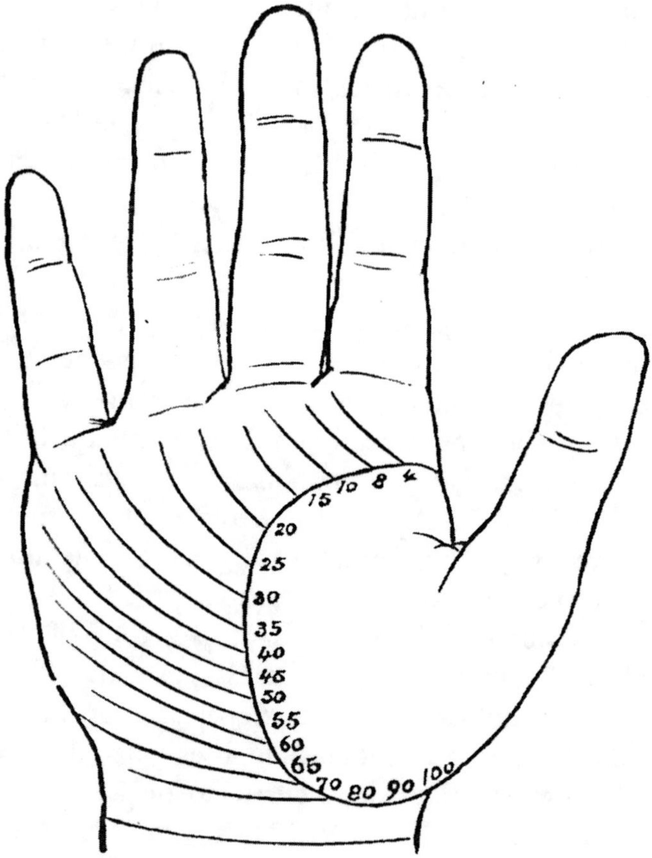

FIG. 10.

THE MOUNT OF JUPITER beneath the Index-finger may mean ambition, honour, religion, love of Nature, and happy marriage; all good qualities, with cheerfulness in social life.

The absence of the Mount means opposite qualities, such as idleness, vulgar tendencies, egotism, and so on. *In excess* we may look for superstition, the excess of religious fervour, pride, domineering tendencies, and so on.

THE MOUNT OF SATURN beneath the middle finger is very significant. Our line of Fate reaches up to Saturn, so Saturn comes to mean Fate. He may indicate prudence and sagacity, or the very opposite, when present. His meaning must be read "between the lines." *The absence of Saturn's* hill tells of misfortune or a wasted existence. *The excess of it* sadness and taciturnity, fear of future punishment, and even suicidal mania; general depression of spirits, with asceticism or morbidness in religion.

THE MOUNT OF THE SUN—Apollo—under the Ring finger, is predicative of taste in the arts; intelligence, genius, and a general tendency to look upon the sunny side of existence. A beauty and grace of heart and mind are present, too, with good religious tolerance and tendencies. A very excellent mound indeed. *In excess* we may imagine whither Apollo will lead us. He will give us a taste for display, for too easy-going manners, for exaggerated tendencies of a warm heart, and exaggeration generally, according to the modifications of the lines of the hands. *Absent;* the Sun's departure will render us cold, content with a material existence, with no taste for art; and, in fine, dull, chilling, and careless of the life we live.

The Mount of Mercury, beneath the little finger, gives us many excellent qualities, and useful withal. He brings us an inventive genius, quickness of thought and action, a working mind, and brain with power to carry out our ideas; industry and commercial tastes, with uprightness in our dealings. Wit and lightness of body are also brought us by this flying deity.

The absence of this hill assures a "negative life," and the absence of all the qualities we have enumerated. *In excess* he is bad. We have the worst side of the attributes; dexterity descends to robbery and swindling, perfidy, lying, scheming, and pretentious ignorance; Mercury, as we know, is the deity of thieves.

The Mount of Mars may be easily interpreted. It denotes courage and coolness in danger, "proper pride," self-control, resolution, and kindred qualities, which are to be found in brave and gentle natures. *The excess of Mars* is not unfavourable, but it may argue violence, even murderous intent, tyranny, and angry passions of the soul. *The absence of the* God of War can be easily summed up in cowardice and unreadiness in danger.

The Plain of Mars is crossed by the line of the Head, which implies the struggle which is continually going on in life, and, while united with the Mount of Mars, the ability to resist them.

The Mount of the Moon closes our list. When it is present it signifies imagination, sentiment, harmony (in music) and a lymphatic temperament, a love of solitude and sentimentality, romance. *Absent*, of course, it means lack of all these qualities. *In excess* causeless worries, despair, restlessness and curious fancies, brain-sickness, madness, &c. The moon is the type of changeability or caprice.

Writers on Chiromancy have divided the hand into three parts, bounded by certain lines. The upper portion is considered the divine part, the centre the natural, and the lowest the material division. The Mount of Venus with that of the Moon unite to form the *Material* portion. The upper part, bounded by the line of the Heart, is the divine portion, and the Natural portion is in the centre, where is the line of the Head and the Plain and Mount of Mars.

We have thus considered the "Mounts" briefly, but we are now only upon the threshold of the Science of Chiromancy as regard the interior of the hand. And with regard to these mountains, we must be cautious in our reading. Sometimes one mount may be much more evident than the others, and then the others are, in a sense, subservient to its influences, and aid it in its ambition or affection, as the case may be. Again, the influence of the mounts must be considered *vis-à-vis* of the lines of the hand. Not only the most evident of the latter, but even the smaller ones, have their significance; so, although it is comparatively easy for a person to read the palm of the hand in large type, as it were, he cannot make a proper book for general circulation unless he employ the "lower case." It is very well for a beginner—like a child—to have a lesson in "capitals," but he must learn the small letters as well.

Thus the palm of the hand is a book to be read

by all who study; but they must study diligently and continuously. There are as many considerations to be entertained and weighed as in a weather forecast. We may and do make broad guesses at the weather, and, at times, are correct; but we have to study the signs. So it is with Palmistry.

CHAPTER III.

OF THE LINE OF THE HEART.

In every hand there are lines of certain depth, colour, and length, and, according to their accentuation, so will the qualities they indicate be more or less present in the individual. We do not say that these qualities will be evident to the ordinary observer, nor even that they are observable at all. They exist in his or her nature, but may be kept in subjection and self-denial by religious training and force of character —in a word, by other lines or mounds. There are some interpretations which are merely traditional, but we will give them when necessary, or advisable, for what they are worth, noting at the time their origin.

There are three or four very important lines observable in the majority of hands. We will take first the three most universal, viz., the line of the Heart, the line of the Head, and the line of Life. These three lines form a figure in the palm of the hand something like the letter M; if the hand be held sideways and with the muscles relaxed, the figure will readily be perceived.

THE LINE OF THE HEART is the uppermost, and we will consider it first. It passes beneath the fingers, and by the ancients was called the Mensal Line, from *mens*, the mind; or, perhaps, from *mensa*, a table, as it appears in the table-land of the hand. But it is now generally known as the Line of the Heart, and is a very important one for us to consider.

There are, moreover, certain indications which we must take into consideration; for instance, the colour, clearness, depth, &c., of the line; and in accordance with these traits, the state of the heart or mind, and the misfortunes which have affected us, may be traced.

To be really good, it ought to rise at the Mount of Jupiter, and cross the hand to what is termed the "percussion" or "striking" part, and be clear, clean, and well-coloured. According to its length we may judge the strength of attachment, and the quality o attachment. For instance, if instead of rising beneath the index finger, the line does not commence until the Mount of Saturn, we may premise a strong feeling of attachment or love, but of a sensual, rather than of a domestic, type.

A long clear line of the Heart, in what may be termed a *Venusian* character, indicates an affectionate and devoted character; but if the prominence be more even under the influence of the Moon, by reason of the Mount of Luna being highly developed, then the line will be somewhat paler, and will indicate more *passive*, if sincere, affection, but will not struggle very long against difficulties, or even against the evils of which the individual's nature is the type or the offspring.

The more this line bears to Jupiter the better it is, and the more it goes over to Mercury, even sometimes turning round to the back of the hand, the more *material* may the affection be regarded as a rule. Jealous persons will find this true, for jealousy is an excess of affection, and therefore a fault. All excess is faulty, "too much" means wrong. Too little of the line of the Heart indicates a martial type of individual, who will gain by violence and not by affection what he wishes. Absence of the line means wickedness, bad faith, and, probably, an early death.

A break in this line may mean weakness, and, consequently, a broken engagement, or a rupture with one we love. According to the place where the break occurs, the cause may be sought. Under Saturn it is "fate;" nearer the Sun, folly; under Apollo, pride; further on, avarice; under Mercury, avarice, combined with ignorance.

Sometimes we find jagged lines or a "chain" on the course of the line of the Heart—these denote inconstancy, flirtation, and intrigue in love and friendship. (Old writers say they argue contempt of women also.)

The colour of the line may also assist us to arrive at a conclusion. If we find it red, and generally good, we may assume strong love—even violent affection—but a broad pale line means the tendency of the nature to dissipation, even to weakness and excess. The pallor of the line indicates the want of power to recuperate fast enough for a dissipated existence.

A sign of death is when the three lines are united beneath the index finger. If in both hands, death by violence is predicted. And if united with the line of the Head under the mount of Saturn, it is also an indication of violent death. But when these lines appear united on one hand, we must always look at the other for confirmation. If the signs are not duplicated, the fatality will, in all probability, not overtake us. Danger may be indicated by the lines, but prudence and training may neutralize the predestined effects; equally as good indications may be neutralized by sordid or unworthy passions if indulged in.

Disappointments in the affections are marked by bars across the line of the Heart; no branches mean a loveless life, so far as the opposite sex is concerned —a withered existence and poverty.

Good fortune is predicted or confirmed by a forking or parting of the line under Jupiter; while commercial or pecuniary losses or deceit are shown by the fall of the line to the line of the Head, and shows the possessor is easily "taken in" in business.

There are other suggestions which will be noticed in time, as they may be connected with the other lines. But we may assume that when the line is broken under Saturn it indicates much susceptibility of temperament; a cessation under Apollo in the right hand means an organization which will devote itself to circumstances, and raise "Bethels" from its "stony griefs." Mimicry finds its *raison d'être* when the line of the Heart ascends the Mercurial Mount, and in actors this will be noticed.

If the line of Heart descend to the line of Head, we shall find the possessor of such a palm letting his heart get the better of his interests, and giving way for love or friendship, which may be tempered by the line on the left hand, showing indications of selfishness in a similar manner.

We must read all the lines carefully on both hands, and strike a balance.

CHAPTER IV.

THE LINE OF THE HEAD.

A REFERENCE to the frontispiece will enable the reader to perceive the line of the Head, and its direction. It commences between the thumb and the fore-finger, and is usually united in its birth with the line of life. But they are quickly parted, one passing across the hand, the other surrounding the Mount of Venus.

The line of the Head and the line of Life sometimes do not commence together. When this is the case, the person upon whose hands this parting is observable will be found to be careless of himself. There is obviously no connection between his or her brain and life, so the individual exists without thought for existence. The line of the Head traverses the plain of Mars, and ends upon the Mount of Mars, with a more or less direct or sloping course towards the Lunar Mountain.

The clearness, colour, length and depth of the line of the Head, indicate in proportion the amount of self-reliance or care for one's own interests which are inherent in the individual. If it rise up to without touching the line of the Heart, the chances are that the person so marked will be of much weaker intelligence in things of the world.

The line of the Head may throw out some branches, and these also possess significance. For instance, if the ramifications extend towards the Mount of Jupiter (index), the sign is that the possessor is easily wounded in his self-love. If such branches seek Saturn's Shrine, they mean legacies or future possessions; if towards Mercury, commercial success; towards Venus, it is a sign that the Head will be easily influenced by love.

Ancient writers used to maintain that white and red marks upon the line of the Head indicated murders or homicides, which have been, or which will eventually be committed. Red points indicate wounds in the head.

When considering this line we must notice its course and tendency very closely, for it is naturally affected by the mounts which it seeks. If towards "imagination," the latter will of course influence it, and a less sound and practical view of life will be arrived at. The fancy will usurp the place of stern reality, and the hues of romance will tinge our views of existence. Lower still into the Moon's territory we shall find a tendency to mysticism; and if the line come right down upon the mount of the Moon, the mount being well developed, it is an indication of, a tendency to, or approaching madness.

So when it turns to the upper hills, it signifies that it partakes of the qualities of those mounts. Mercury thus, as before, means commerce, and so on, as reputation and riches come from the Sun. If it advances too high, it indicates foolishness in connection with the hill it aspires to; that is, pursuit carried to an absurd extent, religious ecstacy, and ridiculous extremes of art, either in painting or otherwise—or less wise.

When we perceive the line of the Head is pale and wide, we look for a want of intelligence or circumspection in worldly affairs. We may, perhaps, find a linked line, indicative of a chain, as it were, instead of the direct and full line we may be led to expect. When this is the case we can point to a want of fixity or concentration of thought; the individual is of the "rolling stone" order, and does not pursue one line of thought or action in a very determined way. So a broken line indicates vacillation.

There are indications of death to be noticed in this line. For instance, capital punishment is foreshadowed upon it; and when we find it divided beneath Saturn (or fate), upon an unlucky hand, we may predict the execution of the individual, which, unless Providence order otherwise, will surely take place. If the hand bearing this fatal sign be otherwise generally fortunate, we can fearlessly modify the sad prediction, and arrive at a less terrible conclusion, such as a broken head or scalp wound of a severe character.

The points of the liar or deceiver are clearly shown by the line of the head, which then appears unconnected with the life, in a divided line, one branch continuing onward, and the other tending towards the mount of the Moon. This shows imagination and deception, a leaning to error and falsehood.

The line of the Head, where shortened in the hand of a sentimental or *Venusian* subject, will argue that he is likely to permit his worldly interest to be wrecked by his feelings; or if the subject be of the masculine order, the sign indicates his impetuosity, and hence his failure in his calculations.

If it descends very much into the hill or mount of the Moon, there is danger of death by drowning or insanity. The Moon rules the water, and a circle at the end of the line is very dangerous.

In considering the line of the Head we must, as will be perceived from the foregoing remarks, look upon the *qualities of the Head* as generally understood, and then translate the signs according as the line is affected by surroundings. A tortuous winding head line, tending towards the line of the heart, will at once tell us that the "subject" is undecided and foolish; that his brain is in danger, and death may ensue. If it, at its termination, unite with the line of the heart, it indicates early decease, or with good signs otherwise may only indicate bad fortune.*

* There are many traditional explanations which we have not embodied in the foregoing indications, and some few conclusions which, if authenticated, are by no means common, and not required in a popular treatise.

Thus the general temperament being first ascertained by the mounts of the hand, and the various influences taken into consideration, we may with success pronounce upon the past and the present, and from them foreshadow the *natural* future. But Providence may overrule all our anticipations; the Soul may achieve a victory over both Head and Heart.

CHAPTER V.

THE LINE OF LIFE.

"HERE," says M. Desbarrolles, "commences the painful portion of the science. At this point we taste the fruit of knowledge of good or evil. Here we learn to read the hands of those whom we love; the finger of death or the life of pain; the loss of sight, or any other affliction which threatens them. We can prognosticate how many years we have to live; and even if we endeavour to put aside the thought by telling ourselves that Chiromancy is not to be credited, the idea haunts us all the same."

The line of Life has already been pointed out; it cannot be mistaken, and it exists upon every hand in a greater or less degree. When it surrounds the Mount of the thumb, long, well-made, with a good colour, the life may be expected to be long and happy, without any great trouble; and such a line means a good character in the individual possessing it.

We may, on the contrary, prognosticate that when the line is wide and rather pale, it, in common with all lines of the same character, has an evil tendency, and bad health, as well as a low type of disposition is present. The student of Chiromancy after a while will also examine the lines crossing the line of life or which pass close to it, and from these things can perceive that illness or accident is likely to arrive at a certain time. How they can estimate the periods at which the maladies will occur may be now explained.

We have given (Fig. 10) a rough diagram of the hand divided into periods of five and ten years (see also Frontispiece). The line of Life is thus divided into a certain number of parts, each representing a portion of our existence, which are marked in the following way. This is by no means a modern idea, but it has been adopted by late writers as well as by the old Chiromants.*

To arrive at a proper period we must have an ordinary compass, and having put one point upon the root of the forefinger and the other upon the centre of the mount of Apollo, describe an arc which will cut the Line of life. The point at which the arc thus described intersects the line of life, gives us ten years, the first ten years of our life counting from the

* This is merely a geometrical rule which has been prescribed for dividing the line of Life. The proper approximate divisions will be found on the Frontispiece, and must thence be mentally adapted to any hand under examination.

commencement of the line below the index finger. For the second circle the moving point is placed between the third and fourth fingers, the next on the mount of Mercury, the fourth curve is drawn from the extremity of the third joint of the little finger at the point where it leaves the percussion, the next circle at an equal distance down the side, and so the next. We have then reached sixty years; the places at which all these circles cut the line of life being marked 10, 20, 30, 40, 50, and 60 years respectively. When the seventh circle has been described, the distance for the eighth must be reduced one-half on the percussion, and we shall thus reach 100 years, the spot where the line of life trends beneath the ball of the thumb.

The reason of this may be briefly explained. If we draw a line towards the ball of the thumb direct from the root of the mount of Saturn, we shall under nearly all circumstances touch the ten years' point. There may be a slight space, but a year or two will make practically little difference, and absolute exactness must not be expected. The line from Saturn, which represents our fate, thus indicates that until we are ten years' old, or thereabouts, we are under the dominion of destiny or fate, and we cannot control our own actions. This will account for the lengthened space in the hand before we reach the first period of ten years.

Subsequently the spaces up to 70 are all equal, because life, under ordinary circumstances, is under control pretty equally up to that time; and after that the life becomes feeble and wearied, so the lines are reduced in length, for then are our years but labour and sorrow in the multitude of instances. In the diagram (*see* Frontispiece) the various periods are marked as a specimen of an ordinary hand, so that any one by careful comparison may ascertain for himself how long he may, under ordinary natural circumstances, expect to live.

[We must again repeat that other lines may have a decided influence upon the line of life; and though the person may actually exist for many years, his life may be practically cut short by illness, and so his want of health may render him helpless. All circumstances and surroundings must be equally balanced; so if a long line be accompanied by a deviation at a certain epoch, extending towards the line of the Head, an attack of the brain from overwork or application is likely to supervene. These are merely warnings written for our instruction and guidance by Nature.]

These facts, then, being kept in mind, we can proceed to the examination of the line of Life, and endeavour to derive some consolation from it.

The line of Life should be clear, well-defined, and of a decided colour. If it entirely surrounds the mount of the thumb and fulfil the above conditions, life will be long and happy; the constitution is thereby pronounced good and the health vigorous.

On the contrary, when the line is broad, pale, and of unequal width in its course, and intersected by other lines, it is a sign of a weakly constitution, even of vitiated blood, and of a succession of illnesses. In fact, the very opposite of the good qualities foreshadowed by the clear, well-cut line.

In the case of the frequent intersections hinted at above, the maladies to be feared will arise from the influences of the portions of the hands whence the cross-lines come. If the lines extend from the line of the Heart, the illness will be caused by the chilling of heart affections or some cause connected with the Heart. If the cross-lines extend from the line of the Head, the disease or malady will be traceable to the brain, or from injury to the head by fall or blows. Lines extending across it from the mount of Venus tell, as may be anticipated, the sorrows arising from misplaced affection or unhappy passion. But if such lines extend from the centre portion of the hand or the plain of Mars, the trials and troubles will come, or have already come, from the struggle with life, commercial losses, or worries of a material nature.

If the line of Life be duplicated (as in Fig. 18), it means a luxurious existence; and if it give the appearance of a chain, or a linked and broken connection, a sad and precarious life may be anticipated or pronounced upon. When this line is seen with roots or branches extending to the mount of Jupiter, it indicates an ambitious nature, not necessarily of a bad description, but one which may honestly desire wealth and honour, after hard and continued labour. In other words, the victory over circumstances gained by pride and will indicated by Jupiter.

If the line of Life be short, the life itself will be brief, and if a decided break or interruption occur during its course, we may expect the occurrence of some serious illness. When, for instance, we find a line broken, as shown in the diagram, page 105, we may at once, and with certainty, conclude that the individual has had an illness which laid him at death's door. But if the illness has already passed, all fear is over, there will be no recurrence of the attack—not of such a violent nature at any rate; *the* serious danger is over. But if broken in both hands it means death.*

In considering the line of Life, we must be careful to examine its appearance and position relatively with the line of the Head which unites with or approaches to it. If these lines join, making a regular acute angle, the prognostication is good, and indicates prudence

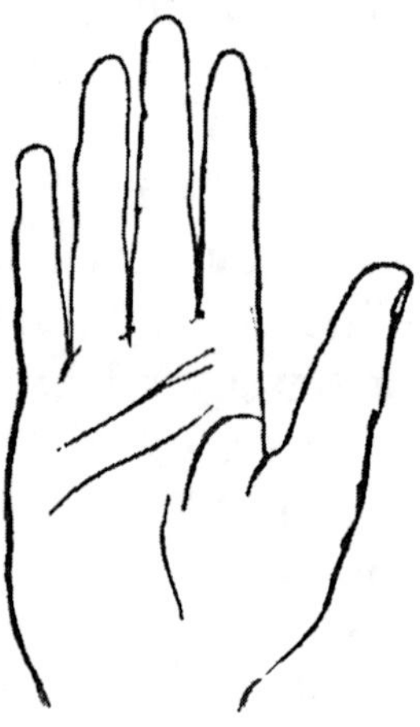

FIG. 11.

and sagacity in business and in worldly affairs, as well as bodily.

If, on the contrary, the lines do not touch it argues want of forethought, "the head will not advance with the life," and projects conceived will be left to wither and die. When a large space intervenes between these lines, it means that the disposition is too frank,

* We may observe that when the lower portion of the broken line tends towards the Mount of the Thumb death is inevitable. If it turn in the other direction there is hope,

and unreflecting in its utterances, or that envy, vanity or even a want of intelligence, perhaps falsehood, are indicated.

If the intervening spaces be very large, and the lines red and strongly marked, the supposition is cruelty, vanity, love of money; or a violent death may be foreshadowed. We say foreshadowed advisedly, for, of course, circumstances will alter cases, and the evil day may be staved off by higher influences, and the evil may disappear.

Again, in a case in which the line of Life and the line of the Head continue for a long time united at the beginning, and do not, as they ought to do, separate beneath the mount of Jupiter (or index) the supposition is that the development of the intellectual life has been naturally slow, or retarded by some means; and that the child has been long in reaching the normal standard of intellect.

If the line of Life unite with the line of the Heart, and also the line of the Head, there is danger of violent death. In this case the influence of the head and heart are considered to be too great for the life and dominate it, leading it into danger. Riches may be expected if smaller lines extend from the line o Life upwards, for our hopes and aspirations point up to dignities; a bifurcation at the point of departure tells us of vanity.

Sometimes little points or circles may be observed upon the line of Life: when these are noticed, they indicate maladies connected with the heart or wounds (*tradition* tells us they indicate the loss of one eye or both). Black spots mean weakness of the heart or consequent dangers.

Connected with the line of Life is the *line of Mars*, a kind of duplicate or secondary evidence of vital force, which may announce success in the camps of Venus or of Mars, ascending as the other indications of the hand point to the tendency of the individual. Sometimes it will accompany the line of Life throughout its course, then riches may be expected or honours. "Sister" lines are usually good omens, unless they appear with bad characteristics, when,

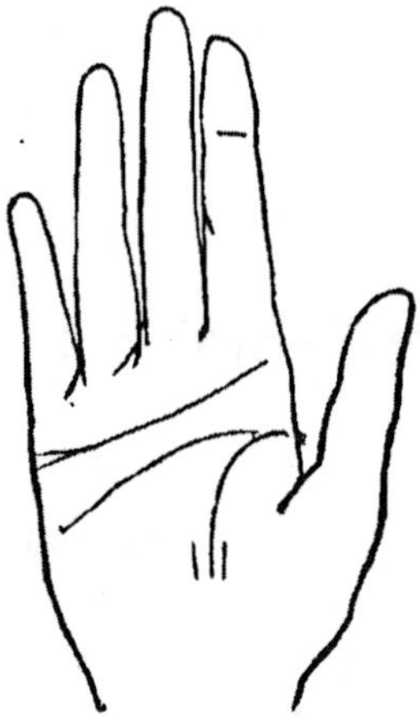

FIG. 12.

instead of alleviating, they only serve to confirm the evil influences of the original line.

There are some tokens upon the line of Life which are best illustrated by small diagrams. For instance, we perceive above, in Fig. 12, a drawing of a hand with two small points, or lines rather, on either side of this short line of life. These symptoms indicate a short life and sudden death. We may also find branches springing upwards and downwards from the line of Life, and they tell us of violent desires and of fading health respectively, as underneath (Fig. 13).

There are other lines sometimes very clearly marked, which arise from the mount of Venus, and cut into the line of life, &c. This is an indication that our destiny is being, or has been, interfered with by Venus (Fig. 14).

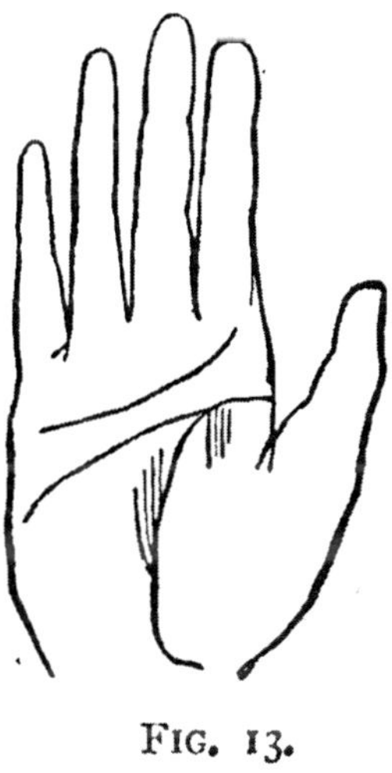

FIG. 13.

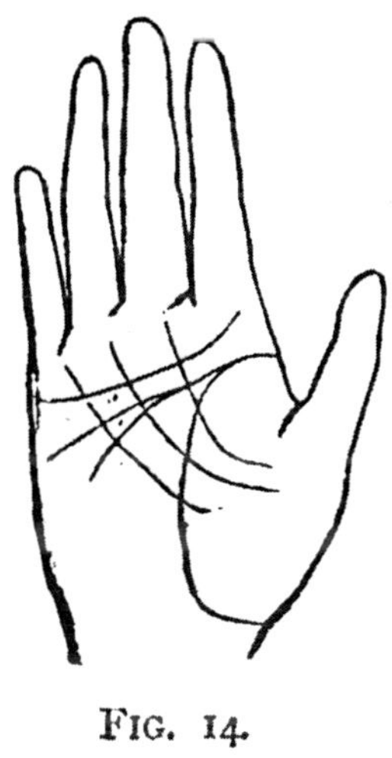

FIG. 14.

To men of letters and those of sedentary and studious habits, we will add a word of warning, even at the risk of having addressed to us the taunt, "Physician, heal thyself." Whenever such a person finds the line of life on his hand parted or bifurcated, he should be cautious in working his brain. Too much fatigue will surely in his case bring on disease or malady of the brain. So let him or her never unduly prolong the tension of literary labour or study. When the work is pressing we are apt to labour unduly, and continue to tax our already hard-worked brain. Our own hand plainly indicates the risk we run in this way. If we ourselves do not exercise due caution, the inevitable failing of health and brain-power will overtake us. The lines distinctly point to a severe illness in our declining days, which will be intimately connected with the brain. The warning will not be neglected, depend upon it; and we would equally advise all our readers, whose avocations necessitate continued application in literary or kindred pursuits, to pause in time, and give Chiromancy the credit which it deserves. We say again, beware!

> "Be warned in time by other's harm,
> And ye will do full well."

A cross at the end of the line of life indicates a good clever man or woman, but one who may, and probably will, love his worldly possessions. Small holes or figures of a dark colour in the beginning of the line tell of murderous tendencies.

We may thus read our characters and probable destiny from our line of Life. Our knowledge of ourselves will be largely increased by this reading of the palm. The knowledge may tend to our unhappiness at first; but if we are wise and take the warnings in time which are written for our learning, we shall, in all probability, be able to avoid the danger, and turn our sorrows into blessings.

CHAPTER VI.

THE LINE OF SATURN.

As fixed as Fate! "There is no use in attempting to alter destiny," say some people. What must be, must be. *Che sarà sarà*, and such-like phrases, indicate the taint of fatalism which is inherent in so many minds. "A man who is born to be hanged will never be drowned," says the proverb; and the phrase may be true *when we find any man who was born to be hanged!* We may rough-hew our destinies, but Providence shapes our ends; and to say that any person, who is a free agent in the world, with a brain and hands, a soul and sense to make his way in it, and into a better one, is *born* to a violent and disgraceful death, is as ridiculous as to contend that Judas Iscariot was destined from eternity to betray his Redeemer. Circumstances, and our own passions *may* bring us to such an end; our unchecked avarice or lust *may* bring us to grief, but we have always a chance, and a loophole for escape. "Fatality" is not to be considered as final, nor incapable of being averted.

These observations have been made because we are about to turn our attention to the *Line of Saturn*, or of fate, or "chance," as it is sometimes most erroneously termed; for there is no such thing as "chance." The indication of circumstances over which we have no immediate or direct control are marked upon

Saturn's line, and here the fatalist will come up triumphantly to convict us out of our own mouth. But we may assure any such that there is no need for "cock-crowing." We plant a seed, and it comes up, but we have no control over the result. We plant seeds in our lives, the crop must come up, the fruit must be reaped, but we need not eat it if be injurious, nor need we continue to plant evil seeds. The soil may be cleared after the first crop; and what is playfully termed our "wild oats," may be rooted up and thrown away.

The indications of Saturn's line may, therefore, as will be anticipated, be various, and the line itself vary in its direction. Its point of departure is irregular, and four places are indicated whence it may spring. It may arise from the line of Life, from the plain of Mars, from the line of the wrist (or Rascette), or from the mount of the Moon, and all this has a meaning; for if we look back and compare the indication of the mounts and lines whence and whither our destiny leads us, we shall find abundant evidence of the tendency of our natures, and the *natural* ending or progress of our lives, *if they be permitted to go on unchecked by good influences.*

The points of arrival of the line of Saturn are as varied as their points of departure. It may cease in the centre of the hand, upon the line of the head, upon the line of the heart, or, again, on the mount of Jupiter, or Apollo, or even towards Mercury. But it usually ends on the middle finger, and thus is called the line of Saturn. Let us consider it, and take the cases separately.

We will, in the first case, suppose the line to rise

from the wrist, and, being of a good colour, clearly marked, rising steadily as far as the first joint, or centre of the middle finger, it indicates unlimited good fortune, notwithstanding all adverse influences to the contrary, particularly if it so appears on the left hand. In the right only, such success will be brought about by *our own exertions* more than by legacies or gifts. Action is in the right hand.

If the line be not so clearly indicated to the middle of the Saturnian finger, we may anticipate obstacles and interruptions in our career, which will depend upon the place or line in which the "Saturnine" stops. For instance, if it disappears at the line of the heart, our interruptions will come from sentimental causes, which will prevent us working for ourselves, perhaps. If it cease in the line of the head, we may fear a sudden shock, or a failure of mind, particularly if the line of Life be bifurcated, as already mentioned. If it extends high up the middle finger, happiness, *or evil fortune*, may ensue in a high degree.

The line may commence faintly and become more clear. This forebodes a better ending of life than beginning. In the contrary case the opposite result may be sought or feared.

If good at the beginning and subsequently tortuous and faint, or even disappearing entirely, it indicates that the happy circumstances of our early days will not continue in after years. A fading in the centre presages troubles in middle life (or if it be cut by other lines); but the end of our days will be prosperous if the line be clear at the upper end.

There are cases in which the line of Fate is altogether wanting—in the Esquimaux we do not find it as a rule. The lives of such people have no particular aims, and though there is no great risk run by them, an accident may suddenly cut them off from their insignificant lives. To such people there still remain the same opportunities for improving their fortunes as for others. It is only by application and work that they will obtain anything. They must remember the proverb, "Heaven helps those who help themselves;" which, however, does not apply to thieving.

We have said that when the Saturnian Line ascends nearly to the first joint of the middle finger, the bearer's lot will be a happy one. This may equally arise from good-fortune, or from bad or evil tendencies *directed by will to a proper use.* Any surplus passion denotes energy, and this need not be directed wrongly. A person may possess a bad hand, full of energy for self-gratification, but if he lead all this into a more healthy channel he will accomplish much in the world —the conquest of self; such a man will most probably succeed in what he undertakes.

When the line of Fate rises upon the mount of the Moon and proceeds directly towards the middle finger it is a good sign, and indicative of fortune likely to accrue from the *caprice* of some one. The reason is, because the moon is the parent of change and caprice. If the line rise direct, with branches tending upwards, it means riches in after-life.

From the line of Life the Saturnian line rises sometimes. This indicates a good heart, and fortune gained by meritorious labour in life. Any cutting lines modify the good fortune, which *may* eventuate in evil. Again, when the finger of Saturn is entered, evil is always to be dreaded, and the higher the line rises in the middle finger the greater is the danger to the individual.

We annex diagrams of the line showing caprice (15), and of misfortune followed by fortune (16).

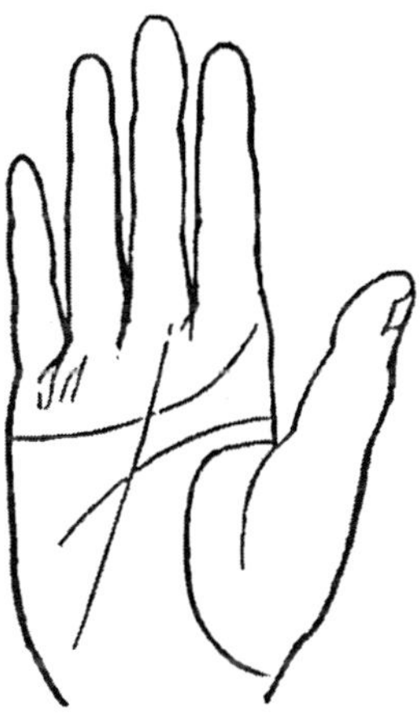

FIG. 15.

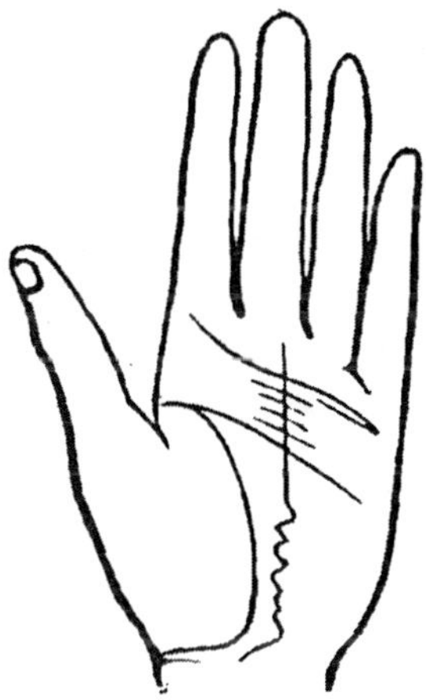

FIG. 16.

When Saturn's line is finally interrupted upon the line of the head or heart, we may expect that opportunity will be arrested by circumstances affecting the brain or the affections; but if it passes through the latter line upwards, it means hard work and travail, or, perhaps, in consequence, a heart broken by despair, and failure of exertion in a good cause.

A double line of Saturn, particularly when the lines are tortuous, means trouble and infirmities connected with abuse of the pleasures of this life. So tortuous lines at the upper end of the line give us anticipations of unrest after a happy life. Pride is indicated by a line passing from the line of the head to the mount of

Jupiter, and if the Saturnine line decline towards it, and is lost in the same place, folly, or even *madness*, may be menaced.

In like manner Saturn's line, when it proceeds towards Mercury, &c., modifies or alters the influence of the mount upon which it fixes itself. Towards Mercury it indicates commercial success, or fame in art and eloquence. To Apollo it is happiness by art or riches, according to the surroundings in which the individual exists. Towards Jupiter, happiness obtained by ambition, and pride of place. Passing (broken) across the plain of Mars we must expect a fight for existence, either moral or physical. So the influence of Saturn is generally adverse, giving a cynical or unhappy tinge to our desires, trouble and toil upon our way.

It would appear, however, that labour to a great extent, or occupation of a useful kind, has an influence also in determining the lines upon the hands, and changes have been often noticed after the lapse of years. If this be so—and there is no reason to doubt it—it follows that the mind and soul have power by the medium of will to modify or reduce the adverse lines upon the hands; and if they can thus alter the lines and indications upon the hands, and in this way show us that "destiny" can be altered, we perceive at once that we have it in our power, after effort properly directed, to improve ourselves, and bid defiance to what some term "predestination" for evil.

We may now rest assured that we have our fate in our own hands, in every sense of the term, and it should be our care to improve our position and vanquish the (evil) tendencies of the line of Saturn.

These tendencies on one hand are confirmed by the other. For example, we know that the "line of chance" may depart from three different places in different individuals, but though it arise from the mount of Venus in the *left* hand, it is merely an indication of a loving or amorous nature, while in the right the same indicates a person determined to carry out his amorous designs at any hazard. In the same way the line setting out from the wrist of the left hand means that in combating the obstacles which we expect to meet we shall be more indolent or thoughtful than if the line appears so in the right hand, which means full *action* in the struggle.

Similarly the line in question, when it starts from the mount of the Moon indicates long journeys, or a desire for them. These, when observed in the *left* hand, show they have been planned; the right palm will tell us of those accomplished. If two branches separate from the Moon and Venus, our travels will be under the influence of the opposite sex, man or woman, as the case may be. In the same way fatal influence of an individual over one of the opposite sex can be guessed when the line of Saturn (in two branches) divides, one branch going from the mount of Venus, and the other from the centre of the hand; the planning and carrying out of such ideas being shown by the left and right hands respectively. When these divisions exist in both hands the will and power to carry it out are both present in the individual.

We may summarize the general signs thus:—

Under Jupiter, thoughts and acts characterized by ambition.

Under Saturn, thoughts and acts relative to agricultural arrangements.

Under Apollo, thoughts and projects for renown in the world of art or literature.

Under Mercury, interested views, or commercial interests.

Under Mars, violence, love of conquest.

The Line of Saturn ceasing at the line of Heart on both hands indicates sentiment and action, which has benevolence for the issue. The left side thinks, and the right hand acts. So its termination in the line of Life means that our destiny will be dependent upon the state of our health.

We may, therefore, regard our destiny from the two standpoints of thought and action; the spirit, or thought influence being shown upon the left hand; the action being indicated upon the right. Both hands must accordingly be inspected, and the lines carefully compared; *most carefully* compared, for a serious error may be easily made, and offence unintentionally given, by a hasty inspection.

CHAPTER VII.

THE HEPATIC OR LIVER LINE AND THE "CINGULUM VENERIS."

THIS line is the barometer of Health. The wire, so to speak, which being "connected" chiefly with the liver—a most important organ—informs us concerning our state of bodily health.

The Hepatic line forms an angle between the line of Life and the line of the Head; in other words, it is the connecting link, or point of contact, between the heart and the brain. In England we all suffer in a more or less degree from disarrangement of the liver at times. The appearance of the line at present under consideration has therefore a wide interest, though it is not to be found in every one. It appertains to the material portion of the hand.

We will now, as in preceding chapters, consider the various appearances generally shown by the Hepatic line, as compared with the others.

The line of the Liver usually rises from the root of the thumb near the line of Life, by the wrist, and passes directly towards the mount of Mercury, and may unite with the line of the Head in the percussion of the hand. (*See* Fig. 8 and Frontispiece.)

If the line commence with or near the line of Life, *without cutting it*, and joins the line of the Head, if it appears well coloured, direct, moderately well-marked, pure and clear, it indicates good health and blood, harmony in the various juices of the body; good memory, success in business, and a good conscience. It also shows that heart and brain are *in equilibrio.*

If, however, it unite with the line of Life it announces weakness of heart; if separated from it, it indicates long life. It may appear winding or undulating; in this case bilious attacks are to be feared, and also headaches, &c., are premised, especially if it be unequally coloured and red when it reaches the line of the Head. A thin and red line of the liver tells us of fever—very highly coloured of brutality or pride; while if it appear intersected and broken, it means weakness of digestion and stomachic affections.

These indications can easily be read by any one for himself. He can easily verify by experience the facts as shown upon his hands. Sometimes this line will be found starting from the mount of Mars; occasionally it forms part of the line of Life; sometimes it will be found ascending to the fingers; when it is not found at all it signifies delicacy of skin, activity of body, and an aptitude for vivacity in speech and conversation.

A cross found upon the Hepatic line is a warning of illness. Ascending well-formed to the base of the little finger it presages long life, while if it be thick and intersected it means old age and failing health therein.

We must be cautious when we find this line uniting under bad conditions with the line of the Head, for such symptoms denote a tendency to brain attacks, in consequence of a too intense application, and they may lead to brain disorders and suicide. Any person, therefore, who finds these signs in his hand must be careful not to overtax his brain by study or work. By the colour and clear cutting of the line the amount of labour and study may approximately be gauged, and the pursuits should be varied when the warning is first heard or seen. "Occasionally," says M. Desbarrolles, "the line of the Liver is accompanied by a sister line," called the "Milky Way" (voie lactée), which rises in the wrist and proceeds to the mount of Mercury. The tendency of this second line is to increase the ardour of love, and when in the hands with the most unfortunate girdle of Venus the indications are decidedly of an evil nature, from a moral point of view.

THE GIRDLE OF VENUS.

We have not much to say concerning this line, for details are quite unnecessary. We trust most of our readers are without it, for its tendencies are certainly immoral. It may be observed between Jupiter and Saturn, and forms a semi-circle ending between the ring finger and the little finger.

It possesses all the evil tendencies of the mounts; false ambition, lying, libertinism, coquetry, for the ennobling influence of the Sun is lost. Fate and the light are in continual opposition, and Venus's girdle is no fit zone for us to wear. It may, however, be found, and the soul may quench the passions; if it end upon the mount of Mercury this will be the case, and energy will quell luxury and sensuality.

As we have already remarked, the mind and religion can neutralize the evil, and the very force which ill-used would bring one to grief, may, properly directed, lead to a better condition of things, even if the fatal zone of the goddess be observable on our palms. The very worst feature is when the girdle instead of turning upwards descends much broken to the root of the little finger in a curve, like a J on its back. We need give no illustration of this figure; it is sufficient to say that in such an individual, unless religious training and strong will turn his mind to higher things, the chances are that his passions will become so ungovernable that he will hesitate at no crime short of murder to accomplish his desires.

At the same time, to have these evil significations the rest of the hand must be bad. The mount of Venus must be high, the outer phalange of the thumb small, the line of Heart chained and pale. It always appears in an intellectual hand to a certain extent, but modified by concomitant signs, for it is only a very crass intelligence that is dead to the charms of passion, and has no appreciation of fervour in affairs of the heart.

We will now leave this unpleasant topic, which we are obliged to mention, and come to the more healthy and pleasant regions of the Sun.

CHAPTER VIII.

THE LINES OF THE SUN AND OF THE WRIST. "MARRIAGE LINES."

We may recall to our minds that the ring-finger (the third) is under the dominion of the Sun, and the mount of the Sun, or Apollo, is situated at its base. This mount is frequently traversed by vertical lines of more or less intensity, sometimes parted or forked. The line—or, in many instances, the lines—are known as those of the Sun or of Fame.

It may happen that the line of the Sun will be found starting from the mount of the Moon, or perhaps from the line of Life; but it signifies celebrity, riches, success in our endeavours, love of art, &c., according to that one of the three "worlds" whence it departs. If it should be found rising from the wrist the prediction will be all the more favourable. It is said that President Lincoln had this line developed in a very high degree, and the fact was pointed out to him that the construction of lines in his hand predicted a violent death, which prediction was eventually fulfilled.

The line of the Sun is indicative of success in life, particularly as to work and art creations. We can, without much difficulty, by considering the starting and arriving points of the line, ascertain in what manner the individual is likely to obtain renown. It may descend upon him as family honour; it may be won by hard work, as when the line leaves the hollow of the hand. It may only signify a good-nature or generosity of character when it rises from the line of Heart.

There are certain forms which this line takes, and much depends upon it. We will give a few indications :—

If the line be clear and deeply furrowed, and opens

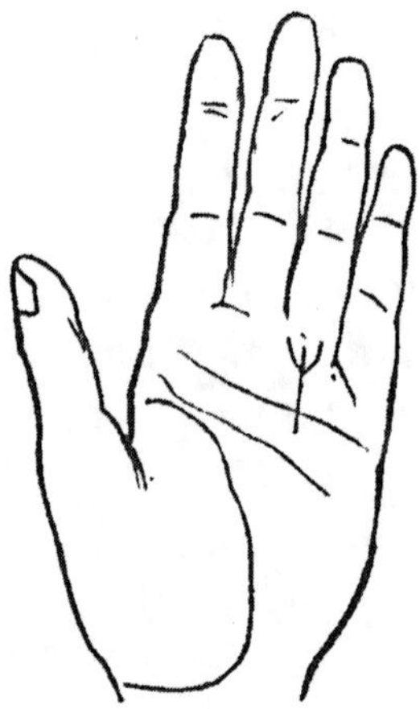

FIG. 17.

up the mount of the Sun "like a ploughshare," it indicates celebrity in art, riches, or the reward of merit, according to the greater or less elevated qualities of the mind, which will influence the body and its actions. It may even elevate the taste of the inartistic.

The appearance of several small lines in the mount mean a great devotion to art and a desire for effect which is carried too far, and has been compared to an arrow shot into space, which is aimed at nothing in particular, and loses itself eventually. Cross lines indicate obstacles, and disappointment in art will probably ensue.

Two or more lines of equal depth may be perceived cutting into the mount of the Sun. If they are unequal and indirect we may expect to find a desire for many branches of art, which tends to make a man a "Jack-of-all-trades and master of none." The sun's face is divided and concentration upon each line is weak; the attempt at too much gives us no decided success in any one direction.

When we find a line dividing like a trident upon the mount of the Sun we have a tendency to riches, glory, and talent; two at least of which neutralizing each other, leaves only wealth perhaps. It may happen that all three fail to arrive at any decided point. So in the case of two lines which separate from the trunk-line and form the letter V, the power is then neutralized by division, and we may entertain a great wish for success, but it will not be realized.

But if we find these branches uniting in a single line upon the mount, and having their rise from the line of the Heart, we may predict fortune from the branch which emanates from Mercury, while the main line indicates glory, and the Saturnine one merit. *Three equal furrows* upon the hill mean great and universal fame when they are of the same form, and ascend towards the third finger with equal intensity.

Lines which invade without actually cutting the line of the Sun mean envious interferences, and consequently bars to the success which we should otherwise attain in due time.

The above are the principal indications of good

and bad fortune imparted to us by the line of Apollo. We find in the hand of the literary or artistic man the three lines running upwards, and the finger has also certain promises of success or failure. The Sun attracts the favour of powerful friends, and many ascending lines indicate the exuberance of "sap" or vital force. When we find the lines of Apollo and the Moon and Venus we have an author's hand, without the latter a critic's.

THE LINES OF THE WRIST.

We will conclude this chapter with a few remarks concerning the Rascette or "bracelets," which will be found in two or three distinctly marked lines underneath the hand. These, with a tendency to rise, mean elevated ideas; if they descend they are a mark of inferiority.

By the number of the lines we can, in a measure, predict the duration of your lives, for every line represents thirty years of our existence. We occasionally, comparatively speaking, find three lines upon the wrist. These show us that, in all probability, we have a long life before us, and that health and wealth await us. This combination of three lines is called the royal bracelet or "triple magic bracelet," according to French writers.

If the lines be continuous, without any break, and of a pure red colour, we may fairly expect happiness in our lives; and considering the possession of health and wealth is indicated by the three lines, it is not an extraordinary circumstance that, granting these two blessings, happiness should follow. There are, however, other conditions which have, in these as in all lines, to be noted and taken into consideration, so even in the apparently simple reading of the wrist lines we must not pronounce too quickly.

Sometimes a chain-like line will be observed, and this appearance usually will be found upon the first line of the wrist. Under these circumstances, we may anticipate a life of hard work; but such will eventually redound to our benefit, for the results will be competency, if not riches, though we shall have, or have had, to work steadily to gain them. M. Desbarrolles mentions a cross in this line as a good sign, and considers, in such a case, a future reward certain after toil.

Long and continuous travel is also foretold or marked upon these lines if they throw up branches which terminate upon the mount of the Moon. It would be interesting to observe the hands of certain "Special Correspondents;" and even commercial travellers might find out either their possible destiny or actual journeys marked upon the lines of the wrist.

There is another condition connected with the lines rising from the Rascette. We occasionally have perceived them crossing the plain of Mars, and proceeding to the mount of the Sun, which readers will remember is underneath the third or "ring-finger." Should this line be present it foretells honours and riches, which may be expected from the favour of some influential personages.

Where a line, rising from the wrist, near the percussion or striking part of the hand, passes up the mountain of the Moon, we may argue from it "tribulation," if it be directed towards the Liver line, and more particularly if the line thus ascending show any irregularity in its course.

[There is an old authority for saying that if a line can be traced from the wrist, which rises upwards directly to the index-finger, the individual will have to undertake long voyages. This statement, like many others of the old students of Chiromancy, must be accepted with caution, and observers must judge for themselves.]

Two branches can sometimes be seen in the line of the Wrist. When this is so, they tell us of a person who will, in all probability, become very rich, and receive many honours and distinction in his old age.

A cross or a star in the angle thus formed is, moreover, a particularly good indication; and one old authority declares he will be healthy, as well as endowed with the world's goods.

Four lines are rarely discernible upon the wrist; when this is the case, the line of Life will be found lengthened, and even doubled; for long and happy existence may be almost certainly presaged for the fortunate possessor. Such people as have these four lines may—unless some specially adverse sign interfere—attain the greatest age at present allotted to mankind, and they will live, probably, till they are one hundred years old.

The right and left hands must be studied in this, as in all other examinations; and if the lines of the wrist are better formed upon the left hand than upon the right, although they may be equal in number upon both, it tells us that we were originally intended for a better existence—that is, that we have somehow or other played with our naturally good constitutions, and our imprudence has, in some degree, reacted upon ourselves.

On the other hand, if the lines appear so upon the right hand more distinctly, or as distinctly, we may accept the token that, by care, we have already recouped ourselves, and that our system is reinvigorated. This is another proof that lines alter in the hand, that bad ones may, by our will and moral improvement, be modified or obliterated to a certain extent; and therefore every one's future, humanly speaking, depends upon his adhesion to the plain and straightforward laws of Nature.

The lines striking out from the wrist: these indicate the tendencies of our nature, according to the mounts towards which they advance. Venus gives us one class; Mars another—the latter a kind of blind bungling into difficulties in our lives, which may swamp us, Mars being the type of the battle ground —as the Moon indicates the water, and, consequently, voyages and travel.

Again, a line from the wrist, ascending to the line of the Head, means a change from an inferior to a superior position in life, and, of course, according to the mount towards which it aspires. If it cut the line of the Heart, and ascend one of the upper and "divine" mounts, this sign is extremely fortunate, and means elevation to certain dignities; for instance—

(1) If it ascend Jupiter, it means success in law or command, and a high position in it.

(2) If it ascend Saturn, the bench of Bishops, or elevation in science.

(3) If it ascend the Sun, literary success.

(4) If it reach the mount of Mercury, it indicates commercial or industrial success, already attained, or in near prospect.

Nor is it difficult to suppose this the case. Granting that our wills, ruled by Providence, impel us to make these efforts, the lines will come, and, unobserved, will quickly indicate the tendency to the wished-for goal.

Furthermore, a line starting from the Rascette to a branch upon the mount of Venus, and extending as far as Jupiter, tells us of a rich marriage, a wealthy alliance; and if a cross likewise appears upon the mount of Jupiter, the match will be a happy one.

But "marriages are made in Heaven," they say. Well, let us endeavour to find what the hand tells us concerning them. If the line end, as said, in Jupiter, a rich marriage.

In Saturn, marriage with an old person.

In the Sun, marriage with a person of artistic tastes.

In Mercury, with a rich merchant, or one whose means are derived from commercial undertakings.

These signs, again, are dependent upon their appearances in the left or right hand. If they appear upon the former, the marriage will depend upon the good offices of a third person. If upon the right hand, the success will be entirely owing to our own efforts or worthiness (*tradition*).

Before closing this chapter, we will give an illustration and a description, after Desbarrolles, of a perfectly *fortunate hand*—a hand, we may add, for the Job-like consolation of our readers, very seldom encountered in this life, perhaps, because perfect happiness, even from a purely worldly point of view, is seldom, if ever, attained. There are, however, many approaches to it, and we trust many of our readers will find theirs a good match. Our own is a sad departure from the perfection here foreshadowed.

We have said in a former chapter, that the girdle of Venus is a bad sign, and so it is in a bad hand. But in the hand here shown, it is present because its affections are directed into a proper channel; and no one will affirm that love, even in excess, when directed to the happiness of one's husband or wife, is a moral fault, particularly as it is in this case tempered by good sense and wisdom. The energy to direct one's goings in the right paths is present, and thus we may make our very faults subservient by the application of a strong sense of right. Self-estraint, or force turned into a good channel, are equally good. The stream may pass its low banks, and overwhelm a village, but if confined within proper bounds it will turn a mill, and conduce to the happiness of the population.

There are, however, circumstances connected with this unfortunate "Girdle," to which, in such a work as this, we must be severely silent.

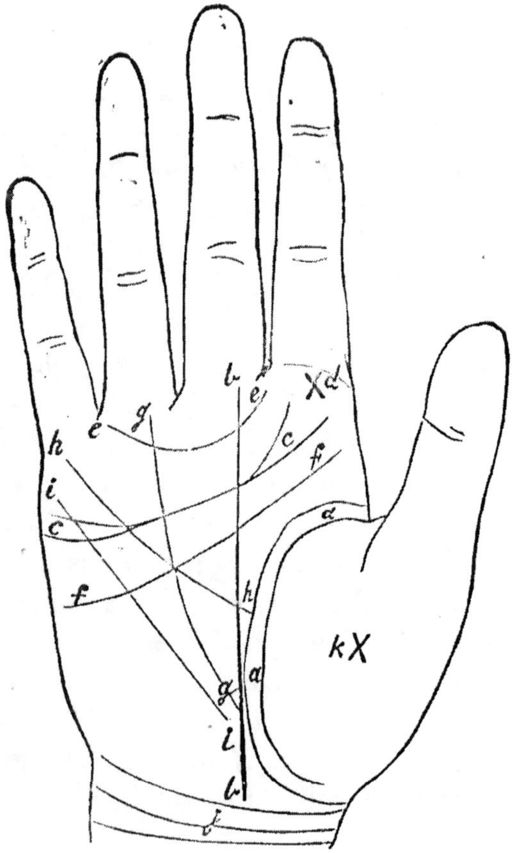

FIG. 18.—A FORTUNATE HAND.

a. Double line of life. *b*. Perfect happiness. *c*. Enjoyment of true love. *d*. Happy marriage. *e*. Girdle of Venus. *f*. Talents. *g*. Art successes (renown). *h*. Perspicacity—fortune and love. *i*. Good temperament. *j*. Long life. *k*. Love for one only.

CHAPTER IX.

ON THE READING OF THE HANDS.—THE DIFFERENCE BETWEEN THE RIGHT AND LEFT.

In the foregoing pages we have briefly, and in no scientific manner, described the various mounts and lines of the hands and their significance, the qualities which may be expected to be found in consequence of their presence. They are the testimony of our lives; the Book from which we may be eventually convicted, unless we eradicate the writing by a change of existence.

We have now, in a short chapter, to indicate the various marks which will, under certain circumstances, be found upon the hand. But we will do so circumspectly. No one will be any the wiser or the worse for our description, though we could warn many a one, were this volume not written for popular and indiscriminate circulation. It may happen that a more scientific treatise will be published, and then those who fear will have their fears either removed or confirmed. Little do we guess how our acts are almost indelibly graven upon our palms. We may forget ourselves, but the writing of Nature is never wrong in our hands, and "the trail of the serpent is over them all."

Let none, therefore, deceive themselves, be they whom they may; the imprint of virtue or vice is as plainly to be read by the Chiromant as this print.

Some very painful instances have recently come under our notice; and while uttering, in these pages, many a warning, we would, at the same time, advise anyone not to be nervous or startled. The marks and lines will fade in the *good* time coming, and, as repentance may be gained, so the mark of the pitch we have touched, and which has defiled us, may be removed.

The whole art of Palmistry is exceedingly simple in *theory*. *Practice* is a different thing; but in a few sentences we can explain the *raison d'être* of the plan, which has probably already been, in a measure, anticipated by those who have followed us so far through the volume. It is simply an observance of the length and formations of lines. We shall soon devote a chapter to this subject. But we can now see how, when a line of Life is short, life is short; when the line is long, life is also likely to be long. When the line is formed in a chain, existence is painful and weary. If the line of Life be pale and broken, we may expect broken health, perhaps breaking spirits, as we pass through the world.

These indications, which every one can understand, are the bases of the Mysteries of the Hand. They are simple enough for a child to read, but the application of them is the difficult problem; and, as in a landscape, we must have all the objects in proportion and our surroundings carefully considered before we make our picture. So in hand-reading we must attend to something besides the principal figures.

Nature gives nothing, unless we take the trouble to seek and inquire for what we want. It is thus all through life. We must dig for coal and iron; we must search diligently for the gold. We must labour in the sweat of our brow for (literally) our daily bread. Nature hides her secrets as the fond mother hides her child's playthings; she tells us where to look, but we must look and search, and probe and learn diligently before we can use the information. So in the readings of the hand.

Now, there are hundreds of honest and sensible people who deride or good-naturedly "pooh-pooh" the Science of Chiromancy, because—and this is the only reason they can give—"it is quite impossible to read such lines." We have—albeit we are not deeply read philosophers—we have read secrets in the hands of men and women which the individuals —people we had never met before, of whose very existence we were ignorant until we were introduced —confessed were true, and known only to themselves. We could multiply instances of this kind, but one will suffice.

A young lady, a few weeks ago, hearing our name mentioned, at a country house where we were staying, came up merrily, and, holding out her hand, said—"Can you tell me anything?" She was a perfect stranger to us until we sat down to luncheon. We looked at her hand, and said, "I see you were engaged to be married, but your pride interfered, you dissolved the engagement a year or two ago, and your health suffered in consequence." She at once withdrew her hand, saying, with a vivid blush, "Quite right; and I *have* suffered; no one but my sister ever knew the real cause. You have told the truth. It *was* Pride!"

Here, then, is an instance—a very simple case, yet it will serve as an illustration. There is no impossibility in the science. The enemies of Columbus told him it was impossible to make an egg stand upright; but he *did* make it stand up on end, and then they saw how easy it was to do it. Before Stephenson made the "Rocket," and even afterwards, railways were derided or feared. What should we be without them? So with electricity. Newton made the greatest discovery ever made by seeing an apple fall. We only claim a fair field for Chiromancy.

But we must remember that it by no means follows that because a person has a certain vein or line upon his hand that he or she is evil-disposed, or likely to reach great honour. All we contend for is a careful examination of both hands, and if we can have our patient behind a curtain, and the hands only visible, we prefer it. For then we have no fear of speaking, and are not led away by any facial expression to doubt the plain evidence of the hand.

In examining the palms, we must recollect that the right hand is usually the more active, and the *initiative* comes first from the right hand; the left will always come to its assistance, however, still it is practically the passive hand. So we seek the more passive signs upon the left hand, and active tendencies upon the right. The indications of thought, as opposed to action, are found upon the left hand.

So if the latter present signs of greater regularity, we may fairly conclude that the individual is of a more passive than active temperament—a man of thought more than of action; a student rather than a player of games. Thus the success of such an one will depend more upon what he will direct to be done than upon what he will do himself. He will conceive the plan, and the execution of it should be entrusted to a "right" man.

Those who possess the most correct and regular signs in the right hand should never wait for Fortune to come to them. Their only real chance of success lies in their rising up and doing—"with a eart for any fate." They must labour and put their shoulders to the wheel manfully. They must win Fortune, or Miss-Fortune will ensnare them. On the other hand, we shall find that those who have the clearer indentions upon the left will succeed, so to speak, of themselves, almost in spite of their passiveness. They will only need "to wait" and not "to labour," particularly if the line of Fate (or Chance) be distinctly and very clearly marked.

These latter are the fortunate individuals who have fortunes dropping into their laps; who having possessions, have numerous presents given to them; who remain quiet and restful, if thoughtful and of indicative mind and mood; who tell others there are burthens heavy to be borne, but will not touch them with one of their fingers. They work with their brain like the Moltkes and the Bismarcks; the others do the manual portion of the toil like the Stephensons and the crowd of labourers in the fields of existence who receive but a scant reward, and then only after hard labour and toil. Look, therefore, to thy hands, oh! reader; to which section of the community dost thou belong?

CHAPTER X.

THE QUADRANGLE—ADVICE TO THOSE "ABOUT TO MARRY"—THE GRAND TRIANGLE.

BEFORE speaking of the little signs which so materially affect the lines and mounds, and, as it were, turn bitter to sweet and sweet to bitter, we will consider the positions and significations of the figures upon the hands as above-mentioned. The first is the QUADRANGLE.

The Quadrangle is that portion of the human hand comprised between the line of the Head and the line of the Heart, and between the line of Fate and the line of Apollo. It is sometimes called the *table* of the Hand, and its form will depend, of course, upon the good—or ill-placement of the two lines aforesaid. The boundaries of this figure are the lines above and below, and on either side of it. Its formation will be perceived at a glance.

If the Quadrangle be regular in its development, wide in the centre, larger by the mound of Jupiter, and wide on the "percussion" of the hand, it denotes a good and straightforward person, an honest and devoted man or woman, good constitution, and good character.

But if, on the contrary, the two lines, *viz.*, the line of the Heart and the Line of the Head are not well placed, or if the former line descend towards the other, or the latter arise to meet the other, it indicates want of decision, timidity, nervousness, and generally want of spontaneity—a retiring character. It may be modified thus :—

Firstly, if the line of the Heart descends far to the line of the Head. In that case it may be accepted that the individual is rather egotistical, and has by looking after his own interests dwarfed his character—or will so dwarf it.

Secondly, if the line of the Head ascend near the line of the Heart, the character may be pronounced good and generous in the main, fundamentally ; but it will be timid and shy, nevertheless, and sometimes maladroit in its manifestations of gratitude, &c. Such an individual will be always hoping to do some really great thing ; to do good and to benefit his fellow-creatures. He wishes to be generous, perhaps, but permits the opportunity to slide past him. *He has no time !* So, by reason of this want of talent to seize opportunity, to "take time by the forelock," he will always be more or less dwarfed in his actions by indecision.

Numerous small lines or signs will frequently be found in the Quadrangle of an irregular and uneven form. A number of lines is a weakness, decidedly. A cross is a disposition to mysticism, if it appear under the finger of Saturn. Superstition is also thus indicated.

A badly-formed cross in the Quadrangle is a misfortune; it may even mean misfortune by worldly elevation. A well-made star in the space tells us of a good man—an honest, well-meaning man—who will nevertheless be henpecked as a husband, and perhaps the plaything of woman if he love her, and so by her dominant influence his naturally good qualities are perverted.

[It is traditionally stated that such a man will be very likely to restore his broken fortunes by hard work.]

A cross in the Quadrangle near the mount of Mars and tending towards the mount of the Moon is (also traditionally) indicative of travel, which, if undertaken, will lead to fortune.

If the Quadrangle be entirely wanting in the hand this is a bad sign, an indication of evil and wickedness.

Thus, by the inspection of the hand any one may determine for himself, or herself, the character of the individual. Any man who is desirous of entering into connubial relations with any woman, may, by attention to the foregoing rules, obtain an insight into his beloved one's character. Similarly, a woman may be informed concerning her *fiancé*; and, while fondly clasping each other's hands, both lovers may all the while be intent upon each other's private and hitherto hidden characteristics, and their chances of success in life!

A fond father may "demand the hand" of the suitor for his daughter's; and therein discover his disposition and tendencies, and his girl's chances of happiness in married life.

The young man may judge of the temperament of his intended spouse, and even of the liberality and designs of his expected parents-in-law. Every man's hand may be against him, and his own hand may be against himself! We cannot always tell for certain, however; the yielding one may by circumstances become as hard as "spongy iron," and yet permit the dropping of good-nature to exude from his heart's pores. The "cross" in the hand may only be the beginning of the lucky "star," and fortune may by industry be achieved!

So let us not play the part of Puck, and separate happy lovers by our whispers. If there be discussions (not dissensions) of the lines of Head and Heart in honest lovers' hands, let them clasp them tighter and decide manfully by patience, pluck, and determination to vanquish Fate together; to combat the portents, to avoid the evil, and *decide at once*, as a first step towards the cure of irresolution, to get married, and do their duty in the state of life to which they may in all honesty be called. So shall they find happiness instead of misery and separation. *Experientia docet.*

THE GRAND TRIANGLE.

This form will be found described in the hand between the line of the Head, the line of Life, and the Hepatic or Liver line, supposing it to exist. In examining the boundaries of the Grand Triangle we must be guided by the direction, form and colour of the lines surrounding it, just as we considered these points in our consideration of the Quadrangle. The evenness, therefore, of the Grand Triangle is a good sign: the irregularity a less good one.

When we find the Triangle regular, we can tell the blood is good and pure, the constitution good in consequence; and, in fact, unless the head and the stomach are all interdependent and yet in excellent condition, health, mental vigour, kindness and spirit, cannot be combined and nicely balanced in such a life or hand.

But if any of these lines be wanting, or if present irregular, intermittent or misshapen, then the individual is wanting in the characteristics connected with the line in which he is deficient. Life, intelligence, health, may each and all be fitful and weak, and even if the man be quite sound upon two, he may be unsound in the third, or weak in all.

So will his life be worried, crossed, and troubled; so will it, perhaps, be a burthen hardly to be borne. The same indication, as already commented upon in the consideration of the Quadrangle, will find place in the Triangle. Troubles *will* rise, and mark themselves in little lines upon men's palms. The worries of his head and in his life will reproduce themselves as indentations upon his hands. As the Indian carries his scalps; as the trapper notches his rifle-stock as a record of the number of his slain victims, human or quadruped; as the schoolboy nicks his "runs" upon his bat, called affectionately "Jehu," because it "driveth furiously;" so will our life-troubles be impressed and cut upon our palms, to remind us in our prosperity that we have seen and overcome the worries of existence. We have passed through the rapids, and are in the smooth gently-flowing stream once for all.

The inspection of the Grand Triangle may be usefully made, when selecting a person for any particular situation which demands coolness, and certain bodily qualities. The head and life must with digestion be in good order, and where a medical examination be not possible, the condition of man for action or command may be estimated with absolute certainty by the Grand Triangle.

By the Quadrangle, the moral and social attributes are distinguished. By the Grand Triangle we can recognize vital and intellectual power, and estimate the duties for which by our condition we are most fitted and most likely to perform to the satisfaction of our employers, our superiors, and ourselves.

CHAPTER XI.

THE LITTLE TRIANGLE—THE ANGLES.

THIS is not always present. It is dependent on the existence of the Liver line and the line of "Chance," for it is enclosed between those lines and the line of the Head. The line of Chance or Saturn ascends through the centre of the hand, bisecting the Grand Triangle. The Little Triangle is, therefore, one-half (more or less) of its greater namesake. When we have considered this Triangle we will speak separately of the *Angles* made in the hand. The Little Triangle should be regular both in the direction and length of its lines. If it be so, and—

(1.) If the Liver line quit the root of the thumb to unite with the Head line, and so form a right angle or nearly, well formed,

(2.) If the line of Fate ascend the centre of the hand directly, and cut the line of the Head at an acute angle, but regularly,

Then the individual is possessed of much intellectual strength and power, and his efforts towards success will, in all probability, be assisted by a concurrence of good luck or fortune.

So by these lines in the Little Triangle we can ascertain probable success in our undertakings, which depend upon brain work for their development. Here again we may, and with seriousness, indicate a way by which parents may ascertain the natural bent of their children's minds and dispositions. Many lives have been rendered unhappy by uncongenial surroundings; and if we can in any way mitigate the probabilities of such very real unhappiness, particularly to young men and boys, we will endeavour to do so.

If, therefore, children have the Grand Triangle formed by the three lines—the lines of Life, Head and Liver, throughout; if these lines are regular, and the Little Triangle, at the same time, exist in the favourable condition just mentioned, such boys may fearlessly be launched upon the sea of Study. They will succeed in it. They are capable of much, and will accomplish much.

But in the absence of these indications in the absence of the Grand Triangle, or in the malformation thereof, such children will not succeed in intellectual occupations, because either the taste for such is not inherent in them, or their natural tendency to idleness will not permit them to apply themselves with sufficient diligence. The presence of much imagination will frequently militate against regular study, and be a bar to a plodding existence. So if the line of Chance be wanting in the Little Triangle, even if the Grand Triangle be well-formed, the liberal professions will not suit the lad so marked; but if their line of "Chance" be wanting, or insufficient, their success may be imperilled by want of forethought.

The Angles which are perceptible in the two Triangles specified in this and preceding chapter, claim a few words. The Great Triangle encloses the Plain of Mars, and has been divided for consideration into three sections containing the angles, viz. :—

(1.) The Upper Angle.
(2.) The Inner Angle.
(3.) The Lower Angle.

(1.) The first is that formed beneath the fore-finger by the union of the line of the Head and the line of Life.

When this angle is acute, well formed and "clean cut," it indicates a good disposition, and frequently nobility of disposition. If obtuse it marks a somewhat dull intelligence.

If the angle commence beneath the finger of Saturn, his influence will interfere with the existence, and Saturn is always a bad companion. In this case, he pre-supposes avarice; or, as old writers assert, captivity.

Again, when the line of Life unites with the line of the Head, lower down still, on the top of the Plain of Mars, it indicates an unhappy life and miserly qualities.

(2.) The Inner angle made by the meeting of the Liver line and the end of the line of the Head towards the Mount of the Moon and the base of the Mount of Mars, if well traced, and of good colour, promises long life.

If very acute, it premises a nervous temperament, and evil associations. If obtuse, we have obtuseness and inconstancy.

(3.) The Lower Angle is formed by the junction of the line of Life and the line of the Liver.

If this angle be well-formed and coloured, it means that our health and our heart are good.

But when very acute it may presage or bear witness to debility, or a desire for money.

If it is thick, and formed of indistinct lines, it indicates a bad disposition; rudeness; even idleness, or inaction generally.

These are the three angles, which should be compared with the lines of the Triangle. We cannot too often repeat our injunction to the reader to bear *all* the points bearing upon the case in his mind when he desires to make a forecast, or pronounces upon a hand submitted to him. Only in this way will his verdict be correct; and he should be cautious, even if he fancy he is quite right. There is no "royal road" to Chiromancy, any more than there is to any other science or study

CHAPTER XII.

ON SIGNS WHICH MODIFY THE PREDICTED EFFECTS OF THE MOUNTS AND LINES.

In the previous portion of this book we have spoken of stars, crosses, and, perhaps, islands. We must, before concluding our summary, say something about these.

The Star (*) on the hand predicts something to come, or which has occurred beyond our own control, and almost invariably indicates *danger.* It is the Red light of Chiromancy; and even if it be turned to our worldly advantage, it will bring in its train some fatality, such as the troubles and anxiety allied to riches, or the worries inseparable from literary or business excess.

The Star may appear on any part of the hand. On Jupiter it means the gaining of our love or ambition. A good "fatality" for Jupiter, we may accept as favourable to our interests. On the first finger-joints, great power and glory as a commander or statesman; particularly on Saturn's (the middle) finger. Under Saturn it is a fatal sign. On the Mount of Saturn it means assassination or execution, according to the interpretation of the lines, &c. Two Stars on the third phalange of the middle finger indicate a shameful death, and may be in consequence of a career of vice.

The star again upon the Mount of the Sun means

riches (unhappy in their arrival); or it may be renown by chance, and unlasting. A line and a star indicate celebrity, in consequence of talent, which has been forced upon one. A number of lines and a star mean wealth.

A Star situated upon the Mount of Venus at the base is evil or unhappiness from the opposite sex.

A star upon the Mount of Mercury is a sign of dishonour. Upon Mars it is death in battle or conflict. If upon the Mount of the Moon it is hypocrisy and dissimulation. But it also indicates misfortune, occurring through the excess of imagination (perhaps trustfulness), and most likely *drowning*, for the Moon is the ruler of the sea.

The square (□) is an indication of force or energy wherever it be may found. It gives coolness in danger, good sense, and the power of "taking in things at a glance," as the phrase is. This sign upon Venus, is, however, unfortunate, and means a convent, cell, or durance vile; and is near the line of Life.

A circle (O) is an indication of glory, as the "halo" behind the head of saints in old pictures is supposed to represent holiness. If this glory mark be found upon the Mount of the Sun, it is an excellent sign; in any of the lines it is a bad one. According to ancient Chiromants, if on the line of Life or on the Mount of the Moon, it foretells the loss of an eye, or, if double, of both eyes.

A point (•), like an exaggerated "full-stop," is a wound, or madness when on the line of the Head. A white point upon the line of the Heart is an indication of conquest in the lists of love; and may mean, if in the Head line, scientific discovery (*tradition*).

An *isle*, or break in a line, as where a stream separates into two branches, which unite again, is generally a bad sign, and often means hereditary maladies. On the Head line it may mean assassina tion or murderous projects; on the line of the Heart, illicit love; on the line of the Liver, going towards Mercury, robbery, or, what is much the same, bad faith in business, or fraudulent bankruptcy. On the line of Life it indicates a mystery of birth. On the line of Saturn it has a curious signification, and yet implies happiness by any dishonourable means, which need not be explained.

The Triangle (△) tells of aptitude for science, and M. Desbarrolles gives us types and examples of this. He says:—

On the Mount of Mercury the triangle means skilfulness in politics (as in Talleyrand).

On the Mount of Jupiter, diplomacy and power greatly developed (as in Napoleon I.).

On the Mount of Saturn, the dark sciences, magic, &c., based upon fear of eternal punishment (Necromancus).

On the Mount of the Sun, science in art (*ex. gr.* Michael Angelo, Leonardo da Vinci, &c.).

On the Mount of Mars, skilful, military combinations (Turenne).

On the Mount of the Moon, reasoning, mystic intelligence (Paracelsus).

On the Mount of Venus, calculation in love (Madame de Maintenon).

The Cross (X) is usually an unfavourable sign, but

upon the Mount of Jupiter it signifies a happy marriage; in all cases this is true. In the Grand Triangle it means religion and superstition, and, if united with the Saturnian line, some good in consequence of religion.

The Cross on Saturn is the bad influence of the planet. On the Mount of the Sun, the Cross signifies effort checked in art, &c., because the Sun is deflected, and things get into a wrong light in con-consequence.

A Cross on Mercury is kleptomania (to use no harsher term).

A Cross on Mars indicates a tendency to strife, and, perhaps, homicide.

A Cross on the plain of Mars, between the Mount of Venus and the Mount of the Moon, means a struggle in life of importance, and a change of position, perhaps occupation.

A Cross upon the Mount of the Moon indicates a liar, who will even use self-deception, and he is not a good character who possesses it, if the lines do not absolve him.

A Cross upon the Mount of Venus is unselfish (single) and fatal love, unless another be found upon Jupiter's hill, when it tells of happy marriage and undivided affection.

A well-made Cross is to be accepted as a good omen, when all its limbs are of equal length. A badly-made Cross is a bad sign; the former adds to the influence of its Mount.

Branches extending from any line are signs of strength and energy upon such lines. Those occurring at the end of a line are only favourable when they *ascend.* They partake of the qualities of their trunks, and upon the line of Saturn are promises of extreme happiness. On the lines of Heart, Life, and Head, they signify exuberance of love, vigour, and health, and of intelligence respectively.

Chain-like formations of the lines are obstacles or entanglements. On the line of the Heart, "flirtations."

Broken or *disconnected* waving lines are signs of ill-luck; and madness or weakness of brain when on the line of the Head.

Parallel lines, called "Capillary" lines, which, after a time unite to make one single line, are a weakness, and indicate an ill-future in a bodily sense. But when there are a great many of these little lines upon a mount, there is a tendency to embarrassment, and they interfere with each other, rendering the result more or less futile.

People who have many rays upon the mount of the Moon are subject to presentiments and such imaginary suggestions. They are of the ghost-seeing class; for the astral fluid in them has a superabundance; and, being in the region of imagination, they fancy they see images, and have forebodings, which arise merely from their own imaginings. To such people we would say—

> ". . . Be ne'er by forebodings deterred;
> But think how oft lives have been blighted
> *By fears of what never occurred!*"

Grating-marks, a kind of beatified gridiron upon the hand, are also considered as unfortunate, and they have special significance. They are supposed to be faults upon the mounts on which they occur, and generate exaggerated qualities, or qualify benefits, according to the hills which they adorn (or disfigure). We need not recapitulate these tendencies; the bars suppose an absorption of the generous fluids, and preserve them in the *material* world of the hand.

Cross rays on the mounts are also obstacles. They interfere with the direct benefits which would accrue from a direct line alone in the same way, as small

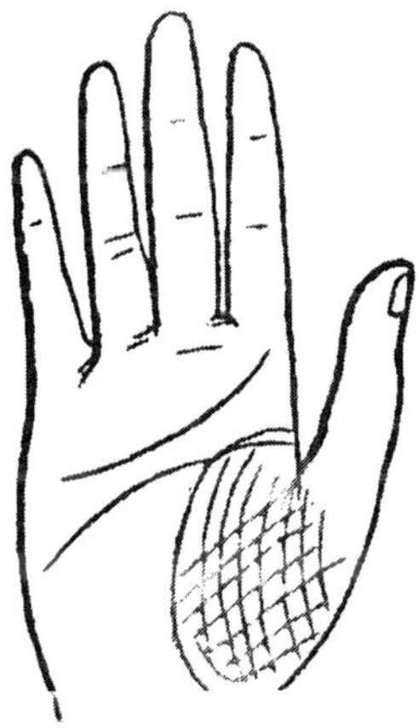

FIG. 19.

lines of a downward tendency are hostile to the main lines whence they fall.

Lines proceeding upwards are good, and intensify the benefits already arising from the line or mount on which it rises. For instance, Mercury unadorned is a sign of commercial intelligence. With one line it shows a "chance" in fortune; if very much "rayed," it becomes robbery, the "chance" being guided by an ill-will to do evil.

Thus, well-placed mounts are good.

With one line they mean success.

With two lines, unhappiness, or evil.

Three lines, at equal distances, *great glory*, success, or happiness.

Tortuous lines, unhappiness and misfortune.

A number of lines, a "choking" of the quality in question.

These are the chief indications which the signs, marks, and formations of and on the Lines and Mounts, as considered apart from the Lines and Mounts themselves, give us, and, even if they are found upon the hand of a child, they do not necessarily indicate evil fortune. The unhappy presage may be averted. The islands particularly are warnings that the ill will most likely come to the individual, but it need not be yielded to and welcomed. By these warnings we can avert trouble, and, by taking due precaution, neutralize it even if it arrive.

CHAPTER XIII.

A FEW HINTS UPON "READING THE HAND." CONCLUSION.

THERE are several things to be kept in mind while the Chiromant is examining a hand. He must, to a certain extent, recognize the character and constitution of his "subject;" he must be able to distinguish his capacity for business; the general condition of his health, and to inform him whether he is idle or industrious; cold or warm temperament; luxurious or envious; liberal or miserly; engaged, in love, or married; whether hot-tempered or good-natured; with many other traits, all of which will be read from the hand submitted, if the student has studied this work. To do this some few instructions are necessary, and the beginner must be *exceedingly careful*, for slips are very easy to make, and no one likes to be accused of faults, particularly when they are unconscious of cherishing them.

First catch your Hand.—Take the left hand in your own as if you were going to shake hands, and holding it loosely thus lying in yours observe its proportions and formations by the light of Chirognomy. This done, turn the hand over in yours and inspect the palm, slightly compressing the sides so as to accentuate the lines. The *feel* of the hand will at once tell you something. Soft hands and rough hands tell tales. The size of the hands, the fingers, the tops of the fingers, the joints, and, lastly, the mounts and lines, must be consulted and taken in almost at a glance. Long hesitation will never do; the quicker the verdict comes, the more penetrating is the sentence, and the higher the estimation of the Chiromant.

(1.) The form of the hand is very important, and here Chirognomy comes to our assistance, as in Part I. The points of the hand being rapidly reviewed, we shall find some indication as to character and occupation, tastes, &c.

(2.) So soon as the *type* of hand has been ascertained, both hands must be examined to see in which the mounts, &c., are best marked. The left hand will be selected, eventually, for line-reading, but we must find out whether the individual is more active or passive, as already explained in this volume.

(3.) The form of the Quadrangle will then be noted, and the character descried by it; and then the Triangles and the Angles must be noted, so as to ascertain the defects or powers of intelligence, &c., as already explained in Chapters X. and XI.

(4.) We shall then have arrived at a very important point. We shall know the social and moral nature, the intelligence and capacity, the aptitude for work, the health and usefulness of the individual. The examination of the mounts at the bases of the fingers will confirm our impressions, for we seldom find many *contradictions* in the hands. We can see modifying traits, but never, or very, very seldom, any contradiction, *per se*.

(5.) The mounts and their protuberances or flatness will tell us much. The mount of Saturn, for example, will inform us whether the person is or is not avaricious, or superstitious, and so on. We need not recapitulate the signs here; the chapters preceding this have dealt as fully as possible with the various indications, and the reader must learn the signs and the confirmatory evidences for himself.

(6.) The principal lines—those of the Heart and the Head—should terminate in a fork, if they be good; *poor* lines end abruptly. The mounts should also be in their proper places, and not lean over to their neighbours. Then we proceed to examine the lines and the stars, crosses, chains, and triangles which intersect, interrupt, check, or mark them.

(7.) The whole palm must be seen and considered. We can obtain an excellent idea of character from the Quadrangle, Triangles, and other Angles, remember; and although the reading of the shape of the hand and fingers is very important, we can tell certain past events from a mere glance at the palm of the hand.

We will conclude with a few sentences respecting the three worlds which are seen and recognized in the hand.

These are the divine or superior qualities of the mind, the qualities of the head, or natural world, and the more material and gross. We will repeat a few indications with reference to the foregoing rules for inspection of the hand, which will serve as examples.

JUPITER gives us pride and ambition, &c.

SATURN gives us prudence, superstition, and sadness, perhaps.

APOLLO gives us glory, riches, fame.

MERCURY is scientific, eloquent, and gives us *finesse* and robbery.

MARS gives us courage, poverty, and resignation.

VENUS gives us love, passion, charity, and fellow-feeling.

The MOON principally imagination.

Let us apply these in excess—

JUPITER, being religious, will, you imagine, if in excess, be very good. He is not. His possessor is simply *proud.*

APOLLO in excess is fond of riches, instead of art, and he will tend to luxury and show.

MERCURY *in excelsis* is simply a thief. . . .

And so on. We shall find excess *bad.* All superabundance is a blemish.

But we must read "with the fingers," as do the blind. We cannot find out the meaning without the fingers, and the pointed, the spatulated, the square, all qualify the mount.

APOLLO with pointed fingers, wish for glory.
APOLLO with spatulated fingers, desire for riches.
APOLLO with square fingers, love of truth in art.
JUPITER with pointed fingers, religion.
JUPITER with spatulated fingers, command.
JUPITER with square fingers, ambition.

We might carry these on to the other fingers, but we have said enough to indicate the view which must be taken of the mounts in connection with certain indications of the fingers. The lines, again, will give us plenty of occupation, and it will be some considerable time, and not until earnest application has been made, that the horoscope will be correctly cast.

There are a great many things concerning Chiromancy which are not written in this book. To do the subject justice, three such volumes as this would not be too many; there are so many interesting combinations, so many scientific facts, so many anecdotes and curious confirmations of characters pronounced, that they would, if written, fill a large volume. But for all popular and amateur purposes, the Chiromant will find the foregoing pages, we believe, perfectly trustworthy. After some considerable personal experience, we have consulted numerous writers, ancient and modern, male and female, upon this fascinating science, which is again rapidly coming into favour. The results of our joint experiences and reading are partly embodied in this volume. The remainder will be added to as experience may decide.

In saying farewell to our public, let us add a little advice to those about to "Chiromant" their friends. Be cautious. Never make guesses. Be perfectly certain, and then do not give utterance to your thoughts unless you feel assured of their reception. We have said all this before, you will retort. Perhaps we have; but we cannot repeat it too often. An enemy may be made for life by an incautious statement; and when the individual has a tendency to murder and homicide, with other angry passions, telling tales in his hand, he may turn and rend you!

As to the future, be particularly careful. It is not "in our hands" in one sense, if it be in another. The marks in our palms are God's warnings to us, and we may pay no more attention to them than we do to Sunday Sermons or Services. Very well. But do not say you had no warning when the axe falls. Be also *very* circumspect with children, their doting parents, and nervous persons. All Evil may be checked by Will and Religion. Strong as the strong man is, Another is stronger, and will prevail.

Finally, do not despise the hand, or its teaching, nor one view of its reality. The marks are there for *some reason;* until you can prove we are wrong we claim to be right! FAREWELL!

THE END.